RHODODENI

CAMELLIAS and MAGNOLIAS
2007

Published in 2007 by
The Royal Horticultural Society,
80 Vincent Square, London SW1P 2PE

ISBN-10 1 902896 70 X
ISBN-13 978 1 902896 70 0

Edited for the RHS by Deborah Parker and Simon Maughan

Honorary Editor for the Rhododendron, Camellia and Magnolia Group
Philip Evans

Editorial Subcommittee
Maurice Foster
Rosemary Foster
Brian Wright

Honorary Production Manager for the Rhododendron, Camellia and Magnolia Group
Pam Hayward

Printed by MPG Books Ltd, Bodmin, Cornwall

COVER ILLUSTRATIONS

FRONT COVER: *Rhododendron arboreum* subsp. *delavayi* – first prize, class 5, at the Main Rhododendron Competition (Species), Borde Hill Garden, West Sussex, 22 April 2006, shown by Mr H Stephens (Michael Shuttleworth)

BACK COVER LEFT: *Camellia japonica* 'Kakureiso' – first prize, class 11, at the Main Camellia Show, Westminster, 11 April 2006, shown by Andy Simons (Michael Shuttleworth)

BACK COVER RIGHT: *Magnolia* × *loebneri* 'Pirouette' – first prize, class 5, at the Southeast Branch Magnolia Competition, Borde Hill Garden, West Sussex, 22 April 2006, shown by Maurice Foster (Michael Shuttleworth)

CONTENTS

Chairman's Foreword

Mike Robinson

'... *the sun doth parch the green...*'
(Henry Howard c.1517– 47)

Quite a year – part delightful, part tedious. Spring was an inspiration: scarcely ever has there been so much flower on our plants, and many shy flowering taxa earned their place in the garden at last. The late start after a cold March delayed flowering until the frosts were over, so the long awaited spring was full of blooms both elegant and pristine. Highlights were the rare *Magnolia sargentiana* var. *sargentiana*, neglected *M. sprengeri* var. *elongata*, fragrant hybrid *Rhododendron* 'Babylon', and *Camellia japonica* 'Kumagai' – a massive single scarlet.

There followed the tedium of dead-heading – I took 500 spent trusses off *R. fortunei* 'Mrs Butler', and even then missed some. I should have been more diligent: deadheading is so much more important if plants are to face a serious drought.

The lack of rain affected gardens in almost all parts of the country, with those gardening on the supposedly ideal rhododendron soil of well mulched Bagshot sand suffering the most. Hosepipe bans, and even worse drought orders, added to the difficulties for those who had not the facilities to store rain water from the winter: it looks inevitable that every gardener will have to invest in these.

Plants drooped and were scorched – or did they? Magnolias here have grown wonderfully, with extension growth measured in feet (metres will not do here) and a truly remarkable seed set, with even supposedly sterile plants such as 'Gold Star' and 'Mark Jury' producing some seed. Only recent plantings needed watering. None of my camellias were watered. That left the rhododendrons – a very mixed lot: anything with *R. calophytum* or *R. praevernum* in it needed almost daily attention. *R. oreodoxa* curled up at the least sign of drought or heat, and all the Neriiflora needed repeated watering. *R. augustinii* needed water but the other Triflora did not. The Irrorata were mixed, but most were little affected even in almost full sun. Many of the Falconera and Grandia suffered badly in the sun from leaf scorch, but *R. sinogrande* did not. Fortunei hybrids fared better, *R. decorum* didn't care, and the Maddenias and Lapponicas weren't watered at all.

Is it worth compiling a list of the less hydrophilic rhododendron subsections and hybrids? Perhaps, when choosing rhododendrons, we should pay more attention to the variation of rainfall in the wild? The articles in this Yearbook on smaller rhododendrons, American azaleas and on Sasanqua camellias are a timely example of plants that will endure relative dryness and heat and sun.

The reaction in the less informed gardening press to the hot summers has been predictable. We shall, of course, be growing nothing but grasses, cannas, and palms from now on. I'd hazard a guess, though, that most of the plants in our three genera will survive the next few decades, but that we may have to wait longer for more discerning journalism.

So for me, at any rate, the summer has been merely boring, with much of each day devoted to watering rather than anything creative, but it has not been disastrous.

What about mulch in these conditions? Mulch keeps down weeds and surface soil temperature, and can look attractive, but does it help in a drought? Mulch does increase the time that the surface soil takes to dry out, but the plant loses much more water by transpiration through the leaves, and a thick layer of mulch may prevent rainwater reaching the roots at all unless rain is persistent and heavy.

The current view about planting trees is that mulch is bad in the early years as it can encourage the tree to put out surface roots instead of sending its roots downwards in search of more sustainable moisture, and that mound planting assists this. Does this apply to plants that are surface rooting in any case? It does seem to work with magnolias and camellias, but what about rhododendrons? We need more evidence.

The Group tour to western Canada and the USA last spring was an inspiration to all who were lucky enough to take part. It is well known that hybridisation of all three genera is thriving over there, and we saw many very exciting new hybrids with spectacular flowers, and equal attention was being given to creating plants with excellent foliage. Also much in evidence was the sheer plantsmanship and the attention given to presentation, companion planting and the collection of species. The lovely garden at Darts Hill is described in this Yearbook: though outstanding, it has many close competitors in the areas we visited. The Rhododendron Species Foundation shows what can be done with the determination to assemble not only a representative collection of species but also to show the variation within each species. There is nothing comparable in the UK.

With the additional virtues of beautiful scenery, ultra-hospitable hosts and superb food, this is an area to be visited again and again.

Equally fascinating was to learn about the approach to collection of material from the wild by Peter Wharton of the Botanic Garden of the University of British Columbia. RBG Edinburgh have a programme in place to return endangered species to the wild, but Peter and his colleagues have gone further. They are providing valuable assistance with the setting up of a national park in the temperate mountains around Fan Si Pan in Vietnam. This involves helping the local people with their aim of creating an economically and ecologically viable tourist attraction. Training is being provided in making sustainable paths into the park, propagation of the species growing there, and assistance with herbarium and taxonomic work. Such an approach is an example to us all.

Members will remember the successful George Forrest study day organised by Maurice Foster three years ago. This spring we are going to repeat the format and study EH Wilson, largely because Mark Flanagan and Tony Kirkham have been retracing Wilson's steps in Sichuan and are beginning to assemble a collection of Wilson plants. Trees, shrubs, herbaceous plants and bulbs will be included. There is a veritable constellation of star speakers but the cost is a mere £15. The venue, as before, is the Lawrence Halls at Vincent Square, and the date is 4 April 2007. Do put it in your diary.

EDITORIAL

PHILIP EVANS

I think it is admitted that, however popular rhododendrons may be with the members of this Group, they are plants generally out of fashion with the gardening public, and more significantly, with the influential gardening journalist lobby. Rhododendrons seem to rate a mention in the press only when they are the (alleged) villain in some some sensational piece of environmental news. We are only too familiar with press castigation of hybrid ponticum (usually generalised as 'rhododendron') as an invasive alien or, more recently, the carrier of 'sudden oak death'. Articles redressing the balance in favour of rhododendrons are rare – but an interesting exception was that by Robin Lane Fox, the distinguished gardening correspondent of the *Financial Times*, on 15 May 2004. He wrote:

'If this column was actionable I think that the rhododendron would have a retrospective claim ...rhododendrons are still remarkably low on the list of gardening columnist's subjects... thousands of garden owners continue to hold fast to rhododendrons and ignore the silence which the major press devotes to them. Increasingly I think the thousands are right.'

Mr Lane Fox then went onto write lyrically about the May rhododendron display at many gardens – Savill Garden, Windsor; Leonardslee; Exbury; Isabella Plantation, Richmond Park; Greencombe near Porlock, Somerset; and in Scotland the RBG gardens in Edinburgh and at Logan. He concluded:

'perhaps you have little space, but a sunny, not too dry and acid soil; I have always loved the low growing rhododendron R. williamsianum *which has bell-shaped flowers in the softest shade of pink and the most enchanting foliage. It is extraordinarily beautiful, even to fastidious eyes.'*

Hopefully the passage above sets the scene for the piece that Peter and Patricia Cox have worked on together for this edition of the Yearbook, entitled *Rhododendrons for the Small Garden* – an innocent enough title masking what I believe is a very important subject. Peter's great knowledge and experience of the genus needs no introduction, and Patricia has had specialised in the design of rhododendron orientated gardens. I hope that via our website and the sale and distribution of the Yearbook outside our membership, their suggestions and advice may do something to break what Lane Fox called 'the silence', and open the eyes of many to what superb foliage and flowering shrubs rhododendrons can be, even in a small and precious space.

Over the period of my editorship, Camellias seem to me to have continued to have the edge in terms of garden popularity – understandably, given their ease of culture and the reliability and invariable beauty of their flowering. Contrarily, in this edition, we have Everard Daniel writing about his experience, in the climate of southeast England, of that much less easy and regular, but fascinating, race of autumn and winter flowering camellias.

Magnolias, although a minority interest, to my mind have increased in popularity considerably in recent years, supported by the greater number of outlets selling a wider range of formerly hard to find cultivars. I am grateful to Jim Gardiner for writing an intriguing piece around a personal favourite – *Magnolia sprengeri* – which provides the excuse to illustrate a selection of the finest cultivars.

If there seems an element of self indulgence in the tone of this piece so far, my excuse is (and this may come as a relief to many) that this is my final Yearbook and therefore last editorial. I have been Honorary Editor of the Yearbook now for 10 years, and I felt some time ago, that this would be the right moment for a change. I have enjoyed the task, and owe a debt of gratitude to all the many authors who have helped me over the years. I would also thank the members of the Editorial Subcommittee for their support. I am particularly pleased that, over the decade, advances in printing techniques have allowed us to afford many improvements in the style and format of the Yearbook.

I am very happy that Pam Hayward decided she could take on the role of Editor, and that the Committee has appointed her. She will bring great enthusiasm and new ideas to the role, and I wish her success.

Arthur George and the Hydon Hybrids

Anne George

Arthur George, breeder of many fine hybrid rhododendrons, was born in South Africa where, as a boy, he enjoyed plant hunting in the Cape. The Second World War ended all that and, after naval training and serving as a navigator in both the Royal and Merchant Navies, he came to England. We married in 1953 and that year were given tickets for Chelsea Flower Show where the sight of those splendid rhododendron displays by Slococks and Waterers rekindled Arthur's love of plants.

He decided that, if he were going to be ashore, then he would take up horticulture, which, with two aunts who were botanists, was hardly surprising. In those days courses in horticulture were few and far between and so the only way to acquire knowledge and gain experience was to work in a nursery. Slococks was nearby and they paid him the princely wage of 2/11d per hour but it was invaluable experience. It was not long before he bought his first rhododendron, the splendid *Rhododendron griersonianum* with its lovely geranium red flowers, but it was the desire to breed these magnificent shrubs that really attracted him and in no time he had hybridised *R. griersonianum* with a good form of *R. ponticum* growing in the garden. Not a very promising cross you would imagine and when it flowered after six or seven years

ANNE GEORGE

Rhododendron 'Springbok'

we were not especially attracted to the vivid magenta-pink flowers, but it was a start and the plant was duly named 'Springbok' (see p.9) for obvious reasons! Well, 'Springbok' itself may not be a show-stopper but it has a good close habit and very nice *griersonianum* type foliage; even so we would never have believed its potential as a parent. Crossed with the best form of the superb Japanese species *R. yakushimanum*, and after another long wait of six to seven years, the first plants flowered just before the Chelsea Flower Show of 1968. Never one to enthuse over his own efforts, Arthur simply dismissed these early attempts, but the ever loyal and enthusiastic Rodney Longhurst (Arthur's right-hand man for over forty years) and I took it upon ourselves to put the two plants, which we thought especially good, on the lorry to go up to Chelsea. Needless to say we were severely rapped over the knuckles but those two plants subsequently named 'Hydon Dawn' (see below) and 'Hydon Hunter' were each later awarded the AGM and 'Dawn' was immediately selected for trials at Wisley. The same cross rendered two more beautiful hybrids in 'Morning Cloud' (now also with an AGM), which was named after Sir Edward Heath's famous yacht and 'Morning Magic' AGM (see p.12) which, when it first appeared at Chelsea, so attracted Lord Aberconway he called it 'Super Yak'! All four have inherited the excellent compact habit and incredibly free flowering character of both parents. Not a year passes without them being covered in bloom. And, last year, 'Hydon Hunter' was the centre of the RHS Garden Wisley display at Chelsea.

To increase the colour range, Arthur's next cross with *yakushimanum* was with

ANNE GEORGE

Rhododendron 'Hydon Dawn' – a very old plant that did many Chelsea shows

'Purple Splendour' and two plants he named. The very beautiful 'Caroline Allbrook' (see below) was named after my mother, who lived to the age of 96, and so we thought hers would be an excellent name for a hardy rhododendron! The companion plant is 'Ernest Inman', deeper in colour and slightly later flowering, both equally floriferous.

Continuing with *yakushimanum*, another cross was made using Slococks' good soft pink hybrid 'The Master' which produced three lovely varieties: two fine whites, 'Concorde', the large blooms with a green eye; 'Desert Orchid' (after that celebrated horse) with perfectly shaped blooms, pink in the bud; and 'Hydon Pearl', with fine soft-pink flowers of considerable substance; all three rather stronger growing up to approximately 2m. In an attempt to get a good red out of *yakushimanum*, Arthur crossed it with 'Shilsonii' and the resulting plant was named 'General Eric Harrison' after another rhododendron enthusiast and breeder, but it has been a little disappointing with an inclination to be rather open growing if planted in too shady a position. However, a cross with the red 'Billy Budd' has been much more successful: named 'Hydon Ben' it has an excellent close habit and bright cherry red flowers, making it an ideal rhododendron for a small garden or even for a pot.

One of Arthur's most attractive *yakushimanum* hybrids is 'Silver Jubilee', a cross with 'Coronation Day', lovely white flowers with a crimson eye, also rather stronger growing, but it is the one Arthur made with that superb species *R. bureavii* which produced 'Hydon Velvet', a truly magnificent foliage plant. The underside of the leaves are covered with rich cinnamon coloured indumentum and the new growth likewise; con-trasting perfectly are the large trusses of pure white flowers in May, making it an ideal plant for all seasons.

Going back now to 1959, one of Arthur's most successful crosses was between a fine Tower Court form of *R. fortunei* subsp. *discolor* and 'Lodauric Iceberg' which produced some excellent late flowering, tall-growing hybrids. The first to be named (in the late 1960s) was

ANNE GEORGE

Rhododendron 'Caroline Allbrook'

'Southern Cross', the large blush pink flowers with a bronze throat, followed by 'Northern Star', even larger white flowers with a greenish throat and both selected for Wisley trials. Others from this cross included 'Starcross', a large scented blush pink; 'Veldstar' a good clear pink, also scented; and 'Gipsy Moth', the deepest pink, named after Sir Francis Chichester's yacht in which he had recently circumnavigated the world singlehanded. Many good seedlings from this cross were too numerous to name and were simply sold under their number '32', and, because they were later flowering and such excellent growing plants, they were in great demand. But this is not the end of the No. 32 story – only last August, we were walking round the nursery perimeter, when we came across a fine tall rhododendron in full flower, its soft pink blooms yellowing in the throat with a red eye which gave it a pale apricot-pink colour. As luck would have it, the label was still readable – No. 32! What could have been more exciting on the 6 August 2005? We have still to think up a suitable name and register it but we want to wait for it to flower again just to make sure it was not a fluke.

Cross number AG 33 followed immediately after No. 32 and was the result of Arthur realising there was a need for a wider range of late flowering varieties and so he crossed 'Daydream' with 'Ice Cream' which created my namesake 'Anne George', medium to tallish growing with a slightly loose truss of salmon-apricot flowers stained crimson, best grown in a reasonably sunny situation to avoid becoming 'leggy'. 'Anne George' made her Chelsea debut towards the end of the 1960s and she was admired by the Queen of Denmark, who was touring the displays with Lord Aberconway. He questioned Arthur about my parentage, but the reply was 'I'm sorry, Sir, I cannot remember' which, needless to say, resulted in much laughter. But it was not until 1990 that 'I' received an Award of Merit.

In 1959, Arthur used a cross made by Roza Stevenson, 'Socrianum' × 'Rima' which he put on to 'Bow Bells', but he had to wait many years before their plants flowered. The best one was named 'Caroline de Zoete', a lovely frilly rimmed pure white with good foliage and habit growing to around 2.5m which received an AM in 1986. If it has a fault it is its flowering time at the end of April, which sometimes results in it being caught by late frost, but still very well worth growing in

ANNE GEORGE

Rhododendron 'Morning Magic' – "Superyak"!

Arthur George Crosses		
Year	Parentage	Cross
1956	*ponticum* × *griersonianum*	'Springbok'
1959	*R. fortunei* subsp. *discolor* × 'Lodauric Iceberg'	'Southern Cross'
1959	*R. fortunei* subsp. *discolor* × 'Lodauric Iceberg'	'Northern Star'
1959	*R. fortunei* subsp. *discolor* × 'Lodauric Iceberg'	'Starcross'
1959	*R. fortunei* subsp. *discolor* × 'Lodauric Iceberg'	'Veldstar'
1959	*R. fortunei* subsp. *discolor* × 'Lodauric Iceberg'	'Gipsy Moth'
1959	'Daydream' × 'Ice Cream'	'Anne George '
1959	'Socrianum' × 'Rima' × 'Bow Bells'	'Caroline de Zoete'
1959	'Socrianum' × 'Rima' × 'Bow Bells'	'Bow Street'
1962	*yakushimanum* × 'Springbok'	'Hydon Dawn'
1962	*yakushimanum* × 'Springbok'	'Hydon Hunter'
1962	*yakushimanum* × 'Springbok'	'Morning Cloud'
1962	*yakushimanum* × 'Springbok'	'Morning Magic'
1962	*yakushimanum* × 'Shilsonii'	'General Eric Harrison'
1962	*yakushimanum* × 'Billy Budd'	'Hydon Ben'
1963	*yakushimanum* × 'Purple Splendour'	'Caroline Allbrook'
1963	*yakushimanum* × 'Purple Splendour'	'Ernest Inman'
1963	*griersonianum* × *discolor*	'Hydon Salmon'
1966	*yakushimanum* × 'The Master'	'Desert Orchid'
1966	*yakushimanum* × 'The Master'	'Concorde'
1966	*yakushimanum* × 'The Master'	'Hydon Pearl'
1967	*yakushimanum* × 'Coronation Day'	'Silver Jubilee'
1967	*yakushimanum* × *bureavii*	'Hydon Velvet'
1967	*russatum* (F25500) × 'Blue Diamond'	'Hydon Amethyst'
1967	*russatum* (F25500) × 'Blue Diamond'	'Blue Chip'
1967	*russatum* (F25500) × 'Blue Diamond'	'Hydon Mist'
1974	'Crest' × 'New Comet'	'Hydon Gold'
1974	'New Comet' × 'Crest'	'Golden Clipper'
1974	'New Comet' × *fortunei*	'Hydon Primrose'
1974	'New Comet' × *fortunei*	'Pamela Robinson'
1974	'New Comet' × *fortunei*	'Hydon Comet'
1974	'New Comet' × *fortunei*	'Hydon Hayley'
1974	'New Comet' × *fortunei*	'Hydon Juliet'
1983	*fortunei* × *pseudochrysanthum*	'Peter Winkworth'
1984	'Dopey' × 'Royal Blood'	'Red Arrow'

ANNE GEORGE

Rhododendron 'Hydon Gold'

a carefully chosen spot. The only other plant to be named from this cross was 'Bow Street' – smaller growing with dainty primrose yellow flowers and, blooming in May, it escapes frost damage.

In 1963 Arthur continued working to produce good late flowering varieties and, using the fine pink form of *R. fortunei* subsp. *discolor* with his original plant of *R. griersonianum*. The best plant was named 'Hydon Salmon', a very distinctive shade of salmon-pink which has proved a most useful addition to the range of late flowering rhododendrons.

Very little work has been done with the blue lepidote rhododendrons, possibly because it was going to be difficult to produce new hybrids which were likely to be significantly different from the already numerous and well tried varieties. However, in 1967, a cross between George Forrest's fine form of *russatum* (F25500; AM 1995) with that most reliable old hybrid 'Blue Diamond' produced three especially good and distinctive new varieties. 'Hydon Amethyst' with brilliant rich violet blue flowers larger than one would normally expect to find on a blue lepidote hybrid and a good, close upright habit, the colour providing a splendid contrast with the more usual lavender shades; secondly 'Blue Chip' another intense violet blue but taller growing and, thirdly, 'Hydon Mist' with large lavender blue flowers and the same good close habit. We grow them all massed together in an area known here as 'The Blue Corner' where they complement each other and look superb at the end of April–early May.

During the 1970s, Arthur decided it was time to breed some good yellow rhododendrons. For a number of years 'Crest' had always been regarded as the best yellow but, although a fine colour, its habit can be too open and so, still using 'Crest', he crossed it with the softer yellow but closer growing lovely Wisley hybrid 'New Comet' produced by Francis Hanger, a truly gifted hybridiser. This cross was done both ways and in 1983 there were some very promising results. Quite superb is 'Hydon Gold' (see above) with clear yellow flowers of beautiful shape, great substance and a good tidy habit. The reverse cross produced 'Golden Clipper' (AGM 1999) with similar excellent fine yellow flowers but taking on the more open habit of 'Crest'.

A year or so later, still using 'New Comet' but with the very good *R. fortunei* from Tower Court resulted in the soft primrose yellow 'Hydon Primrose', again with great substance and good habit; it was an instant hit but we made the mistake of overselling it and the stock has never recovered! Another lovely plant coming from this cross is 'Pamela Robinson', named after a good friend who has bred as many fine dogs as Arthur has rhododendrons and was, until recently, a Crufts judge. This very attractive variety takes more from *fortunei*, the soft pink flowers with a greenish throat, lighter green foliage and an excellent sturdy habit, nice and bushy growing to approximately 2.5m. Also from this cross, is 'Hydon Comet', another good, warm yellow with a large rounded truss but the flowers are emasculate. 'Hydon Hayley' and 'Hydon Juliet' are two more which are closer to *fortunei*, their flowers in subtle colours, 'Hayley' lilac-pink with a yellow eye and 'Juliet' a soft creamy-apricot named after a friend in the Loire Valley, a splendid cook who used to entertain us to the most delicious lunches! Other good yellows which were crossed with 'Hotei' have yet to be named and registered because they suffered badly in recent hot dry summers, but hopefully there are some survivors.

Another interesting cross dating from this period, which Arthur made, was with *R. fortunei* and the species *R. pseudochrysanthum*, one seldom used in hybridising – which is surprising considering its good compact form and distinctive foliage. The results have been very rewarding, taking the best characteristics from both parents. Only one plant has been named to date which is 'Peter Winkworth' after another good friend who is an avid rhododendron enthusiast and creator of a superb rhododendron woodland garden, in between being a highly successful breeder and trainer of horses. 'Peter Winkworth' is an excellent sturdy growing, compact plant with masses of blush pink flowers in May which turn to white when fully open, making it an ideal garden plant.

ANNE GEORGE

Rhododendron 'Red Arrow'

Finally, the last Arthur George hybrid I shall mention is 'Red Arrow' (see above), the long awaited, truly superb scarlet, a cross between 'Dopey' and 'Royal Blood' which takes its good close habit from 'Dopey' and brilliant colour from 'Royal Blood'. Flowering well into June, it is especially useful.

Although I shall not go any further, I can say there are many more promising hybrids in the pipeline. Having spent many years sharing in the excitement awaiting the flowering of a new hybrid, the joy when it looks promising and the disappointment when it fails, I realise only too well that when you embark upon the breeding of rhododendrons one lifetime is not sufficient!

Anne George is the wife of Arthur George, and for 40 years worked for the leading antique porcelain company in England, latterly as Managing Director. In retirement she devotes herself to the Hydon rhododendrons

Magnolias, Mostly From Seed

Tim and Ray Thornton

This short article describes our efforts at growing magnolias, mostly from seed, to furnish an empty garden acquired in 1976.

While most of the magnolias in British gardens were obviously grown from seed originally, one hears little about the results obtained from the many seeds which are distributed annually by organisations such as the RHS to amateur growers such as ourselves. What happens to them? The results we have obtained from growing magnolias from a variety of seed sources may encourage others, and we hope this article may be the tip of the iceberg, as we have many other seedlings of interesting origins, yet to flower.

Origins

When we moved into our house there were few plants in a garden of over two acres, due to the property's former use as a small riding stable, and plant material of all kinds was urgently needed, although our daughters immediately requested, and got, horses of ever increasing size. Thus trampling of small seedlings by escaped horses was a real risk although no magnolias are known to have suffered this fate, but rhododendrons were not so lucky. Soil was mostly New Forest gravel (acid) but overlaid in some places with clay 'topsoil', brought in when the local recreation centre was being built. Certainly there were no magnolias in the garden, just the inevitable *Rhododendron ponticum*.

Two of our articles in earlier Yearbooks have described efforts at growing rhododendrons from seed. Magnolias were thought about from the start as companions to the serried ranks of rhododendrons being planted and a few expensive purchases of Asiatic magnolias were made, but some hot summers, including 1976, saw them off before they became established. These included *Magnolia campbellii* 'Betty Jessel' and a very small plant of *M. mollicomata* 'Lanarth', purchased for what seemed an enormous amount of money, £16, from a well known local nursery. If only they had survived! There was, however, one notable survivor from these early years, from which we learnt quite a lot. A plant purchased as *Magnolia* × 'Iolanthe' flowered after a few years, but did not seem to be identical to the plant with the same name in the nearby Hillier Arboretum at Romsey. As the years progressed it became apparent that it was definitely not named correctly and we thought it might be 'Ruth'; but we now think it is an unnamed hybrid of *M.* × 'Lanarth' from New Zealand. It is now about 25 feet high. We soon found out that misnaming of magnolias in nurseries was not that uncommon.

In 1982 we stayed in Falmouth. The first sight of Cornish gardens with their tree magnolias in full flower triggered off the desire to return to them as desirable garden plants. We were particularly impressed by Caerhays Castle, Trewithen and the semi-wild garden at Penjerrick. Later we became acquainted with Peter Chappell on a visit to 'Spinners', and over the years his enthusiasm for the genera, and specific magnolias, has rubbed off.

At a later date still enthusiasm increased after a visit to Darjeeling, India and the sight of the elderly plant of *M. campbellii* 'Darjeeling' in the Lloyd Botanic garden in full flower. Then we visited New Zealand and the Jury nursery in Taranaki.

Some plants were purchased in Cornwall in 1982, although we did not at first realise the potential confusion between seedlings and grafted plants of particular cultivars. One, allegedly *M.* 'Caerhays Belle', has still to surprise us by actually flowering, and has been overtaken by seedlings. Because of the expense of grafted plants, growing magnolias from seed, or even by micro-propagation, was then considered. After attending a conference on the latter subject it was decided not to pursue this option, especially as we were advised to start with the excised tips of immature seeds. At a later date we started grafting magnolias ourselves, but this assumes a supply of suitable understocks, and, of course, scions of the desired magnolia.

The likely timescale for the production of flowering plants exercised our minds considerably. We realised that Asiatic magnolias can take up to 25 years to flower. Assuming the purchase of a two- to three-year-old plant, we would first have to wait for it to flower and we could see that we might have to wait about 30–40 years to see the results of a deliberate cross, although the

RAY THORNTON

A cross by John Carlson: *Magnolia* 'Robin'

behaviour of 'Philip Tregunna' *(Magnolia sargentiana* var. *robusta* × *M. campbellii)* in this garden gave us much encouragement. Purchased as a small plant, it first flowered some five years after planting and has flowered every year since.

We also had little idea of the success rate in producing plants worth growing and naming. One is often told to grow 100 plants from each rhododendron cross, but clearly the prospect of growing 100 of each magnolia cross cannot be entertained. Observation of seedling magnolias in Jury's nursery indicated that, in practice, ten was a more realistic number for us, and fortunately often only a handful of seeds germinate anyway. Nevertheless, we are still swamped by magnolia seedlings at various stages of development.

Some compromises were clearly necessary, preferably involving obtaining magnolia seeds from exchanges or by acquiring some friends with nice magnolia gardens. In

RAY THORNTON

Magnolia 'Black Swan'

fact, we have had enormous help and friendly advice from both sources. The Magnolia Society and the RHS Rhododendron, Camellia and Magnolia Group provided seeds, as did a number of private gardens. This has inevitably led to an ad hoc approach and a somewhat random selection of parents, but the presence of an Asiatic tree magnolia somewhere in the pedigree was preferred.

We started growing from seed in 1983 and a reasonable number of plants have flowered in the subsequent 23 years. Many, of course, are still to flower. Most of our rhododendrons are named after the Short 'C' class flying boats that flew from Southampton Water. The magnolias are named after birds, with some consideration for the origins or characteristics of the plant. However, local aeronautical connections have been brought in by another route. The 'Spitfire' first flew at Eastleigh Airport, Southampton in 1936. Rolls-Royce piston engines were named after birds, and the two used successively in the aircraft were 'Merlin' and 'Griffon'.

Cultivation

We consulted all available books on growing magnolias from seed, and especially *Asiatic Magnolias* by the late GH Johnstone of Trewithen. In the Northern Hemisphere, seed usually becomes available in late October/early November. The orange coating was removed and seeds stored in damp vermiculite until January, followed by a regime of some six–eight weeks stratification at around 2–5°C, unless the seeds had started to germinate in transit, when they were sown on receipt. Seeds frequently germinated well, on rare occasions they came up the following year. Immature seeds collected in September also germinated well.

There was nothing special about growing on; the trouble starts later. Plants were potted on and moved to a polytunnel for the next two–three years, depending on the rate of growth. There is then a choice: plant in autumn and risk frost damage the following spring, or plant in spring and risk drought the following summer. Either is a risky strategy in Southern Hampshire, more so in the last few years. On the whole we opt for spring planting, with the plant at a height of three–four feet. Watering may well be needed for the first summer, and for later ones too. In the rare event of a wet spell, slugs are a great problem, climbing up the stems and eating the young shoots. In the early days we sprayed

RAY THORNTON

Magnolia 'Cornish Chough'

sulking plants with foliar feed to get them moving, as recommended by the late Sir Peter Smithers, but more recently plants seem to grow quite freely – we leave them to their devices, and a little water, or sometimes a lot of water.

New magnolias

The first batch of plants were derived from a cross of *M.* × *veitchii* 'Isca' with *M.* × *soulangeana* hybrids, and were therefore 25% *M. campbellii*. One plant from this batch was extremely vigorous and grew away ahead of its siblings. This produced very large flowers of nearly pure white and has been named 'Avocet'. Another plant of this cross was subsequently named 'Snow Goose' and is a purer white than 'Avocet'. Some plants of this cross are still to flower some 24 years later, and are getting ominously large!

Next we tried *M. mollicomata* crossed with *M.* × *soulangeana* 'Rustica Rubra'. Only one plant seemed worth naming as 'Cuckoo', and is now some 25 feet high, covered in the expected pink flowers, and with a very long flowering season.

John Carlson, of Gwent, in Wales has been hybridising for many years, generously sending his seed to a number of magnolia enthusiasts. Five seeds of his cross between *M.* 'Pickards Ruby' × *M.* 'Caerhays Surprise' produced only one seedling. This produced fat flower buds in 2004 and 2005, on quite a large tree, but each year the frost got there first. Even in 2006 there were frosts around at the time of flowering. But eventually we could see flowers of a very dark maroon-purple *(RHS Colour Chart* Red/Purple 59*)*, opening to a water-lily shape. We have named this one 'Black Swan' (see facing page).

Another cross made by John Carlson was between *M.* 'Star Wars' and *M.* 'Forrest's Pink'. This produced an extremely attractive floriferous small magnolia named as 'Robin' (see p.17).

Returning to the big Asiatic magnolias, seed of *M.* 'Caerhays Belle' (ex-RHS seed list) produced a very fine hybrid with large pale pink flowers with some subtle striping. We have named this one 'Cornish Chough' (see above).

M. sprengeri var. *sprengeri* 'Diva' × *M. sargentiana* var. *robusta,* purchased as a small plant at a Cornish nursery, was probably correctly named and produced a plant with extremely large flowers in a clear shade of pink, named as 'Osprey'.

For later flowering hybrids we have flowered two seedlings of *M. sieboldii* × *M. hypoleuca*. Both have large scented flowers appearing in June: these two are named 'Merlin' and 'Griffon'.

Finally, there are our attempts to produce a yellow flowered magnolia. We have many yellow cultivars in the garden, the actual flower colour ranging from cream to pale yellow. The darkest we have in this group is 'Honey Liz'. Seed was obtained from various sources, including the late August Kehr – although his seedlings have yet to flower. Seeds of a *M.* × *brooklynensis* cultivar were obtained from the Magnolia Society, and two plants resulted. Whether these are F2 hybrids, or arose after pollination with another magnolia, is not known, but the first to flower has surprisingly uncrumpled and dark yellow flowers, with green overtones, *(RHS Colour Chart* Yellow Orange 14), from a green bud, and named as 'Greenfinch' (see opposite).

We now have a garden with ever increasing numbers of magnolias which are getting steadily larger. The horses finally departed about three years ago, although we have left part of the garden unplanted. Inevitably we have also bought a fair number of other people's magnolias, but provided you take a long-term view, some spectacular plants can be produced at minimum cost, providing you can allocate many hours of time to nurture them.

RAY THORNTON

Magnolia 'Greenfinch'

Acknowledgments

We would like to thank particularly the following for advice, help in various ways and the gift of seeds for new magnolias, most of which are yet to flower: John Carlson of Pontypool, Gwent; Peter Chappell, Spinners Garden, Hampshire; Michael Galsworthy and his Head Gardeners, Trewithen Garden, Grampound Road, Cornwall; Nigel Holman, Chyverton Garden, Zelah, Cornwall; Rachel Morin, Penjerrick Garden, Falmouth, Cornwall; Jeremy and Felicity Peter-Hoblyn, Lamellen Garden, St Tudy, Cornwall; and Malcolm Pharoah, Marwood Hill Gardens, Barnstaple, North Devon.

Dr Ray Thornton is a member of the Group and his garden near Southampton has an extensive collection of magnolias and rhododendrons. He and his son Tim (Dr T.J. Thornton), joint author of this article, share a a great interest in magnolias

A Very Strange Rhododendron

Mike Robinson

Expeditions to the north of Vietnam in the early 1990s found an unexpectedly large number of rhododendron species on the mountains near the Chinese border. In spite of these being at lower altitudes and latitudes than related species from Yunnan, many of them have proved to be hardy in much of the UK, and represent valuable additions to horticulture. This article deals with one of the 'big leaved' species from that area.

First reports[1] suggested the presence of *R. sinofalconeri* plus two other species from either subsections Falconera or Grandia. Keith Rushforth suggested the presence of a species similar to *R. protistum* var. *giganteum*, and seedlings matching *R. protistum* var. *protistum*. The difference between these is the presence of an indumentum entirely covering the leaf underside in var. *giganteum*, and an indumentum absent or confined to the area near the leaf margin in var. *protistum*, and one must assume that this is what was observed in the wild.

He also reported the presence of a species growing among the ones described above which had a pale brown indumentum, and suggested this was from subsection Falconera, mentioning that it had cup-shaped hairs.

Following a further visit, he[2] revised his opinion, suggesting that there are three possible species – a species resembling *R. sinogrande* from subsection Grandia; *R. sinofalconeri*; and a third which might be a hybrid of the preceding two, and mentioning cup-shaped hairs on a plant with the indumentum characteristics of *R. protistum*.

MIKE ROBINSON

Rhododendron AC431

David Chamberlain's current opinion[3] is that other than *R. sinofalconeri*, there is only one 'big leaved' species in Vietnam.

So much for the reports from the wild: what of these plants in cultivation?

I know of three people whose plants from either KR1986 or AC431 (see previous page) have flowered: the corollas are almost white, ventricose, and similar in form to, but smaller than, *R. sinogrande*.

However, it is the leaves which are of especial interest: they have juvenile foliage markedly different from adult foliage, and the transition between the two, which, in my plant, was followed the year after by flower formation, is abrupt.

The juvenile foliage is very large – I have seen a plant growing in ideal conditions at Eckford with leaves almost a metre long. The leaves are chartaceous, markedly wrinkled, and curved in two dimensions. On the youngest plants the leaf undersides are almost glabrous and, as the plants grow, many leaves show the classic 'round the rim' indumentum of *R. protistum* var. *protistum*: in later years the indumentum may spread to form a thin but uninterrupted covering.

The adult foliage is much more similar in appearance to a typical member of subsection Falconera. The leaves are flatter, usually smaller than the juvenile leaves, the upper surface is dark green and somewhat shining, and the indumentum of the underside is matt, pale brown, and continuous over the whole lamina.

On neither type of leaf have I been able to find the rosulate or the cup-shaped hairs which define subsections Grandia and Falconera. The indumentum is unistrate and of dendroid hairs only, so strictly the species fits into neither of the subsections; it is closer to subsection Grandia, in which some species have dendroid or ramiform hairs.

The presence of juvenile foliage with varying amounts of indumentum appears to explain the reports of two big leaved species (in addition to *R. sinofalconeri*) in Vietnam. It would seem there is but one new species allied to the big leaved subsections in this area. The allocation of this species to a new subsection may be justified, but that is a matter for the botanists. I do hope, however, that it will be given a Vietnamese name.

It is interesting that a new species from the same area, closest to *R. arboreum* subsp. *delavayi* also has dendroid hairs only[4] and also lacks the expected rosulate hairs. Tracing the evolution of this characteristic, if it were possible, would be fascinating.

I believe the phenomenon of juvenile foliage differing in characteristics other than indumentum covering is unique in subgenus Hymenanthes.

References

1 RUSHFORTH K, *Rhododendrons with Camellias and Magnolias, RHS, 1993*, pp. 40–41

2 RUSHFORTH K, *Rhododendrons with Camellias and Magnolias, RHS, 1998*, pp. 37–38.

3 CHAMBERLAIN DF, private communication

4 MCQUIRE JM, private communication

Mike Robinson is the Group Chairman and gardens in East Sussex

Rhododendron AC431 Subsection Falconera aff.

A partial description from a plant in cultivation in East Sussex.
Collected by Alan Clark in 1992. In the wild a large shrub or tree to 12m growing in mixed broad-leaved forest below the summit of Ben Khaong, Lao Cai province, Vietnam, 2300m.

Young growth: sparsely pubescent with dendroid hairs.

Leaves:
JUVENILE FOLIAGE Leaves elliptic to oblanceolate, 20–70cm long, 10–24cm wide, *chartaceous, markedly rugose,* curved in 2 dimensions; upper surface glabrous; under surface glabrous or with a pale marginal or partial indumentum of dendroid hairs.
MATURE FOLIAGE* Leaves elliptic to slightly oblanceolate, 20–35cm long by 9–16cm wide, coriaceous, not rugose, flat or slightly concave, apex rounded, base obtuse, not decurrent on the petiole; upper surface dark green and somewhat shining, midrib impressed, primary veins 16–18 pairs slightly impressed, very sparsely pubescent with dendroid hairs covered with a transparent colourless secretion; under surface with primary veins prominent, covered with a *persistent suede-like unistrate indumentum of pale brown dendroid hairs* which form a continuous matted canopy; petiole curved, round, not grooved, 2–4cm. long.

Inflorescence: a racemose umbel of 15 flowers, rhachis 5.7cm long, sparsely tomentose.
PEDICEL 4.2–5.3cm long, densely floccose with long white hairs.
CALYX 8–10 lobed, an elliptic undulate rim, 7x9 mm, lobes about 2mm long, outside sparsely floccose towards the pedicel, eglandular.
COROLLA broadly tubular-campanulate, ventricose, 4.5–5.5cm long, 4–4.8cm in diameter, *white* with a slight ivory tinge, fleshy, glabrous on both surfaces, lobes 8, 1cm long, 2–2.3cm across, overlapping, rounded, emarginate, the 2 or 3 upper lobes with maroon basal flashes up to 1cm long.
STAMENS 16 or 17, unequal, 1.4–2.4cm long, shorter than the corolla, filaments sparsely puberulous at the base; anthers dark to pale brown.
GYNOECIUM about 3.2cm long, shorter than the corolla.
OVARY a slightly truncate half ellipsoid, 1cm long, 7mm across, densely floccose with transparent colourless hairs, eglandular.
STYLE 2.4cm long, curved, glabrous, eglandular.
STIGMA a flattened dark elliptical disc 4x2mm.

*Note: There is an abrupt change to the production of mature leaves, which developed on my plant after approximately 12 years, followed by a flower the following year.

Autumn and Winter Flowering Camellias in Southeast England

Everard Daniel

Walking up from the valley at Wakehurst, 'tis Spring as I luxuriate in the glorious sight of a low-growing pink camellia in full bloom. But looking round, the fresh breeze is rolling red and yellow maple leaves across the lawn and the convincing illusion is broken. It's a mild afternoon in early November, and plenty of autumn colour to see, but what other flowers are at their peak? Well, only the earliest of the Mahonias. Such is the value of the sasanqua camellias.

Yet they have only recently started to be more widely grown, despite the great popularity of spring camellias. Part of the problem is that they flower after we have finished our garden-visiting season and we miss them at their best. Also, they grow well in shade but need more sun and warmth to flower profusely; they are more popular in Australia and California. So they are often recommended for growing on warm walls where they do well, but do try them in an open site; and remember, they are tolerant of near-neutral and heavier soils. The finest plants I know grow on walls of buildings in Leonardslee Gardens in Sussex, near the Gift Shop, where several truly magnificent varieties have reached the second floor gutters. Interestingly, these plants flower very well, even though they do not get full sun; it suggests that flowering is much more reliable in mature plants. *Camellia sasanqua* leaves are smaller and narrower than *C. japonica* and the growth habit is generally more open and informal; they are vigorous growers, throwing out long, flexible stems which are ideal for training. Alternatively, they can be cut back and pruned into much tighter, more formal bushes and used like many another evergreen in garden design, but far more interesting!

The flowers are smaller than most spring camellias and many are single, with distinctive splayed stamens. In many double varieties, some or all of the stamens have become petalloid, giving an anemone-form flower. The flowers shatter rather easily, so they do not cope with rough weather, and transporting to shows is nearly impossible. The petals drop individually and so the bush never has untidy dead flowers. They all have a distinctive musty scent, so surprising when we first encounter the sasanquas, after all the scentless spring varieties.

Their origin is Japanese, where about four species grow wild and they are separated in common parlance, with 'sazankwa' being the autumn-flowering and small-leaved and 'tsubaki' the spring-flowering larger-leaved camellias. To us gardeners in the West, they are *C. sasanqua* and *C. japonica* respectively. Good to see the common and Latin names so linked; but *C. sasanqua* is just as Japanese as *C. japonica*.

The Japan Camellia Society shows 200 varieties in its book *Nippon Tsubaki – Sasanqua Meikan* (the Nomenclature of Japanese Camellias and Sasanquas). Their cultivation in Japan goes back to at least the 14th century, so parentages are inevitably somewhat speculative. Many of the sasanquas we grow are of hybrid origin so we need to know the parents. *C. oleifera* is the Chinese equivalent of *C. sasanqua*. Then there is *C. hiemalis*, of uncertain, possibly hybrid origin. Some say it is *C. sasanqua* crossed with *C. japonica*, others that it came from China to Japan as a bonsai type, so might it be *C. oleifera* × *japonica* ? (*C. japonica* does also grow in China). Yet others argue it originated in Japan and was taken to China...

Whatever its origin, it often gives richer colours, later flowering and low-growing habits to its hybrids. This is called the winter sasanqua or cold camellia, 'kan tsubaki' (not to be confused with the Snow Camellia, *C. japonica* subsp. *rusticana* which is the hardier form of *C. japonica* and grows further north and in higher hills in Japan. We probably know this one best in the hybrid *C.* 'Arajishi' with its distinctively dark, glossy and serrated leaf. But that is spring, and I have digressed...)

Then there is another obscure one, *C. vernalis* which as its name suggests, is really a spring one, but whose genes are mixed into the winter-flowerers. This may also be *C. sasanqua* × *japonica*. As neither *C. hiemalis* nor *C. vernalis* are found in the wild and as both are possibly hybrids, it does seem sensible to bracket all under the sasanqua umbrella, though you will find them separated in the *RHS Plant Finder*.

The *RHS Plant Finder* lists 79 sasanquas available in the UK, many of which were bred in the USA and Australia. So what do we grow in southeast England? Most widely, *C. sasanqua* 'Narumigata' (Narumi Bay in Japan) which is a single white with a pink rim to the petals (see next page). It reminds me of dog roses or apple blossom, but larger. It is one of the ones growing spectacularly up the walls of buildings at Leonardslee. Alas that they start to flower just as the gardens close at the end of the season. There were also several perfectly shaped young bushes about 2–3m tall, sadly now gone, in the Savill Gardens; I suspect waterlogging one winter killed the roots. Buying this variety out of flower can be interesting – be warned, there is a surprising range of different clones being sold under this name. I believe the true clone to be cupped and to have one of the largest flowers of any sasanqua. Others should perhaps be called 'Rainbow', 'Setsugekka' or 'Fukuzutsumi'. It is sometimes still grown by the old, incorrect name of *C. oleifera*, which is the Chinese species.

Those of you who have travelled to warmer climes for your winter breaks may well have seen magnificent bushes of this variety, and out there they set viable seed quite readily. These have been used in Japan for centuries. The oil squeezed from these black shiny beads is said to be fragrant and of superb quality for cooking. The old fashion was for long hair anointed with the oil. Alas our plants do not set much seed in our cool winters.

There is a whole range of other varieties available in whites, pinks from blush to rosy-

EVERARD DANIEL

Camellia sasanqua 'Narumigata'

EVERARD DANIEL

Camellia sasanqua 'Plantation Pink'

red and some true reds, though few. They also show most of the flower forms, from the commonest single to semi-double and peony/anemone double. Formal doubles are rare. I resist the urge to describe each and every one as such listing articles seem tedious, but a general guide to favourites may be of use.

Of the singles other than 'Narumigata' (see above), there are a couple of reds that are popular. Hilliers put 'Crimson King' on the map a few years ago; my plants disappointed until they got to 1m last year. 'Yuletide' gets its photo in all the papers, but please don't fall for it as demand outstrips supply in the nurseries and it is like gold dust. Single whites are good, especially the upright, strong growing 'Kenkyo', and 'Baronessa de Soutelinho' is a very little known one on the walls at Leonardslee which also impresses. In pink, there are 'Rosea', 'Plantation Pink' (see above) and 'Papaver', and also the rightfully very popular 'Hugh Evans' which always seems to set twice as many buds as any other – you get your money's-worth. 'Variegata' is an outstanding foliage plant with silvery variegated leaves which go so well with the white, flushed pink flowers.

Of the semi doubles, the pink/red hiemalis hybrids 'Dazzler', 'Bonanza' and 'Kanjiro' (see p.27) are all strong upright growers with larger flowers. In Cheshire one year, plants of 'Kanjiro' were a great delight to guests arriving on Christmas Day; however the flowering time of all sasanqua types does vary significantly from year to year. 'Kanjiro' was grown incorrectly as 'Hiryu' until recently and may still be found under that name. The true 'Hiryu' may well not have reached us yet. It is said to have *C. vernalis* blood and 'Yuletide' is a chance seedling from it. 'Kanjiro' has the vigour and soil-tolerance that makes it a useful and widely used rootstock for grafting such as the *C. reticulata* varieties that won't root from cuttings.

Varying from semi-double to almost peony is another strong upright grower called 'Sparkling Burgundy' in rich pink (see p.27).

EVERARD DANIEL

Camellia sasanqua 'Kanjiro'

EVERARD DANIEL

Camellia hiemalis 'Sparkling Burgundy'

The best I have seen was growing in John Hilliard's garden in Crawley and it had formed a 3m tall open small tree, growing in clay on the south side of the house.

One or two varieties are very low growing, almost prostrate. The plant I began this article with at Wakehurst is 'Showa-no-sakae' and it is almost a groundcover, several times wider than tall, and ideal for a bank or over a retaining wall. I would love to see it grown among large rocks by a waterfall. 'Showa Supreme' is an improved version, a chance seedling from it and very similar in habit and flower.

There are two new groups fairly recently introduced and showing promise. Bob Cherry owns the Paradise Nurseries near Sydney and has been breeding camellias for years. Some 15 of his are now listed in the *RHS Plant Finder*; all named with the prefix 'Paradise'. Several have quite large flowers; 'Paradise Little Liane' is a very dainty white with some of the smallest leaves of any camellia I know. In Maryland, USA, Dr Ackerman has bred many fine camellias, including his 'Winter's' camellias of which 6 are available in the UK; examples are 'Winter's Snowman' (white) and 'Winter's Toughie' (pink), both strong growers with semi-double flowers.

Crosses between sasanqua and spring camellias generally produce early spring flowerers. The best for my mind is Howard Asper's cross with *C. reticulata* varieties to produce 'Dream Girl', 'Flower Girl' and 'Show Girl'. Only the last is available and I would love to meet the other two. There is a good plant of 'Show Girl' in the Valley Gardens, from a distance resembling 'Donation' in size and shade of pink, but in full bloom much earlier; when you get closer the flowers are clearly semi-double with the splayed stamens and scent of sasanqua. The petals often roll lengthwise.

Lastly, honourable mention should be made of one or two other camellias. There is a lot of interest in growing *C. sinensis*, not so much for its tiny white flowers in November, but rather as the tea bush, whose dried leaves fill a billion tea bags every year. *C. japonica* 'Gloire de Nantes' and 'Nobilissima' often have their first flowers by Christmas and so can be recommended in big tubs and brought into the conservatory for the coldest months. *C.* × *williamsii* 'November Pink' is one of the originals from Caerhays Castle in Cornwall and will often live up to its name, so much so that I have found it being confused with pink sasanquas.

All the plants I have mentioned should root quite easily from cuttings, either semi-ripe in summer or with bottom-heat in winter. Sasanquas can be very slow to grow away though, and some people say that fertiliser in the compost may be the problem. An occasional weak liquid feed may be the answer.

For further reading, Stirling Macoboy's *Colour Dictionary of Camellias* and later *Illustrated Encyclopedia of Camellias* are excellent and I must gratefully acknowledge the inspiration, joy and help these books give me. *The Nippon Tsubaki – Sasanqua Meikan* (the Nomenclature of Japanese Camellias and Sasanquas) is also well worth seeking out for its good colour photos of 2,200 *C. japonica* and 200 *C. sasanqua*. The text is in Japanese; English text available in separate paperback.

Everard Daniel is a longtime member of the SE Branch of the Group

Rhododendrons for the Small Garden

Peter and Patricia Cox

Nowadays the choice of rhododendrons suitable for the small garden is enormous, whether species or – generally easier to grow but not as interesting – hybrids. Because a garden is small it does not mean that all the chosen plants have to be small-growing. A variety of heights is so much more pleasing to the eye and even more important is the foliage which being evergreen in most cases, is there the year round. Perhaps the choice should be made out of flower so that the flowers do not distract from the foliage. However, this may not be practical if devising a colour scheme of harmony when in flower.

It is most important to make sure that the plants will be reliably hardy for your area. What does well in the milder coastal areas may not be suitable inland, in the north or in a frost pocket. Look out for hardiness ratings, either on the label or in a reference book or if ordering from a reliable catalogue, hardiness ratings should be stated. Different hardiness ratings may be used, we prefer H1–5, 5 being the hardiest, but some sources may use just H1–4. As most smaller rhododendrons come originally from high mountains with cool wet summers, some are not able to tolerate the high temperatures and dry conditions experienced in southeast England and flourish much better further north. Thus some shade is needed for even the smallest leaved kinds in the south, contrasting with full sun in the cooler, damper parts of the north. An open north-facing site is desirable as it delays and prolongs flowering and allows the soil to retain more moisture.

There is a general rule that the larger the leaf, the less exposed a site needs to be. For really dwarf plants, a low hedge, or equivalent in height such as *Phormium* (New Zealand flax), is adequate for wind shelter, even in an exposed site. Where shelter is better and a bed is to be reasonably large and a feature in the garden, choose two or three taller ones for the back, to flower later than the front group. Those small ones in front could be planted in groups of say three to allow them to grow into each other to form a dense clump, thus eventually covering the ground and stopping annual weeds from growing. It is not a good idea to plant single specimens in grass which competes with the rhododendron roots, takes away the possibility of mulching and the weight of a lawn mower compacts the soil, all of which can have a devastating effect on the rhododendron roots and growth.

Should you wish to plant rhododendrons in a mixed border remember to allow enough space for them to develop to their expected width and do not allow the foliage of bulbs or perennials to lie on top of their leaves, resulting in them being smothered and causing dieback.

Good soil conditions are a must. Ideally the soil should be free draining, friable and rich in organic matter. 100% organic matter or nearly so is not a good idea as it will eventually break down into too fine a texture and either become dusty in dry weather or a sludgy mess when wet, leading to root rot. Fine peat should be avoided and never used for mulching as when it dries out, it repels water. Composted conifer bark or needles, shredded conifer trimmings or beech or oak-leaf mould make the best mulches and may also be used to mix into the soil. Raised beds can be highly desirable, especially if your natural soil is heavy. Two parts of any or a mixture or some of the above with one part sharp sand or fine grit and one part light loam makes an ideal mixture. This gives especially good conditions for rhododendrons that are wholly or partly epiphytic in their natural habitat. This means they grow up in trees, on rocks, very steep hillsides or ridges. With the threat of higher temperatures and less summer rain in the future, varieties with epiphytic blood in them could be invaluable as they are much more drought tolerant than rhododendrons that grow naturally in the ground. Many epiphytic species have large scented flowers but their drawback is that the majority are tender. Present and future breeding should lead to varieties that are hardy enough for most areas, drought tolerant and have scented flowers.

Recommended varieties fit into several different groups according to height and width, medium sized or small leaves and then sub-divided according to whether they are species or hybrids or to colour. We include medium growing species with excellent foliage the year round, one or two of which will easily fit into a small garden.

Rhododendron pachysanthum (see below) with medium sized leaves and height and width of 2–3m, is a hardy and easily grown species from the island of Taiwan with outstanding foliage with persistent silvery to brown indumentum on the upper leaf surface and thick woolly indumentum on the lower surface, at first pale, turning to a rich rusty brown. The flowers which appear in March–April are white to pale pink, usually with spots. Equally good and hardy is *R. bureavii* which may grow somewhat taller in a

PETER COX

Rhododendron. pachysanthum

very favourable situation. The leaves are dark green and shiny on the upper surface when mature with thick, rich rusty-red indumentum below, which is so beautiful when the winter sun lights up the underside. The flowers are white flushed rose in April–May. Another great foliage plant which is usually under 2m is *R. campanulatum* subsp. *aeruginosum* which in selected forms has glaucous-blue young foliage, retaining this colour for most of the year. This looks particularly well with blue meconopsis. The well-known *R. degronianum* subsp. *yakushimanum*, best known as just *R. yakushimanum* or 'yak' for short, is almost too good to be true, forming a perfect dome wider than high in an open situation though it can eventually reach over 2m in partial shade. With its dark shiny leaves, covered with loose white indumentum at first, and pale rose fading to white flowers, it is still a must for every garden, despite its multitude of hybrids which never equal it foliage-wise.

Rather different for foliage effect is *R. orbiculare* with bright green rounded leaves on a mounded plant if grown in the open, setting off its pink to rose mid-season flowers. An apparent relative is a startling newcomer from south China but seemingly hardy species with the unfortunate name of *R. yuefengense* (see below). Only introduced four years ago, most seedlings flowered freely at three years old. The round leaves are thicker and darker than *R. orbiculare* and the pale pink flowers do not open until June. Described in *Rhododendrons of China* Volume 3, it is said to only reach 1.5m but is obviously much wider than high. A stunning plant to look out for in a few years time.

'Yak' hybrids are now so numerous that it is hard to select a few of the best. One rivalling it for foliage is its hybrid with *R. pachysanthum* of which there are two similar clones, *R.* 'Viking Silver' and *R.* 'Glendoick Silver', both with pale flowers. These have the most silvery foliage of any 'yak' hybrids. Many of the best 'yak' hybrids were raised on the Hachmann Nursery in Germany and the next two are amongst their finest. *R.* 'Fantastica' has large trusses of two-tone pink flowers, deeper around the lobes. *R.* 'Lampion' forms a low mound, covered with light red fading to creamy pink bells. Two of our favourites raised elsewhere are *R.* 'Harkwood Premiere' with pale lilac flowers

PETER COX

Rhododendron yuefengense

fading to white with a reddish-purple blotch and *R.* 'Ken Janeck' with thickly indumented leaves and large pink flowers that also fade to white, creating a good contrast. Later flowering is *R.* 'Dopey', a really good bright red with full trusses. *R.* 'Percy Wiseman' has plentiful peachy cream flowers, one of the easiest to grow. The last two will grow to over one metre. All are free flowering.

Another group of species suitable for the back of a border are those of the subsection Triflora. Although all might eventually grow too tall, the advantage that these have is that they can be pruned as and when desired. All are exceptionally free flowering and can be kept quite narrow if space is severely limited. *R. yunnanense* can be either white or pink, marked olive to crimson. *R. oreotrephes* has a neater habit and has the advantage of glaucous foliage, very striking in the clone 'Blue-calyptus'. *R. augustinii* has as near blue flowers as any rhododendron in its best forms though these tend to be a little tender. All flower in April–May. To start the flowering season really early, plant *R. dauricum* 'Midwinter'. This can grow to 2m plus but also it stands pruning and most years can be picked in bud to open for Christmas. It has bright rose purple quite frost resistant flowers and is more or less deciduous.

R. williamsianum is a super plant in its own right and it also has masses of hybrids which tend to keep its roundish leaves and bell-shaped flowers. While most are hardy, some, including *R. williamsianum* itself, come into growth when there is still a danger of frost, so a cold site is better avoided. The species is very compact, naturally forming a mound or dome, often wider than high and can reach 1.5m high and more across in time. The lovely pink bells open in April–May. The majority of its hybrids grow larger and more open. *R.* 'Gartendirektor Rieger' is one of the tallest with large cream spotted rose flowers. *R.* 'Linda' is more compact with frilled rose-pink flowers. We are raising new hybrids with crimson-black to reddish foliage to rival *Pieris* although we have not quite got as far as to equal the bright reds of the young growth of some selections of that genus. So far we have named *R.* 'Ever Red' with shiny crimson-purple leaves and flowers of a similar colour and *R.* 'Wine & Roses' with green upwards pointing leaves, crimson on the

PETER COX

Rhododendron 'Graziela'

underside and masses of rose coloured flowers. Both are compact, not likely to grow higher than 1m and flower in April. These are a real breakthrough for unusual and striking foliage.

R. 'Graziela' (see facing page) is another plant with very different, eye-catching very narrow leaves. It is hardy and easy to grow with an abundance of rose-purple flowers in May and is good with creams or yellows.

Dwarf reds mostly come from the parentage of *R. forrestii* which forms prostrate mats and has comparatively large tubular-campanulate flowers in March–April. While this is easy enough to grow in thin woodland on banks, it needs full light to flower freely and does not like excessive heat or sun. Despite these drawbacks, we would never be without it. Its hybrids are more accommodating. The widest grown was *R.* 'Elizabeth' until powdery mildew attacked it; now it is not worth attempting. *R.* 'Scarlet Wonder' is still one of the best, with plentiful bright red flowers in May and only grows to 60cm. We like *R.* 'Dr Ernst Schale' which is even more compact with lighter red flowers. *R.* 'Carmen' has good dark foliage and deep red waxy bells, a gem. A relative of *R. forrestii* and the other parent of *R.* 'Carmen' is *R. sanguineum* subsp. *didymum*. This makes a neat little plant with dark green leaves and blackish-crimson flowers that do not open until June–July. Unlike most of its relatives it flowers freely from a very young plant.

Some connoisseur's plants of subsection Taliensia are often the pride and joy of rhododendron species specialists. They may take ages to flower but the foliage is something special. Low and generally compact is *R. proteoides* with small, narrow recurved leaves with a thick rufous indumentum, with occasional pale pink spotted flowers while *R. pronum* is also compact with glaucous young leaves with fawn indumentum. Both are slow growing and plants for a lifetime. Generally rather taller is *R. roxieanum* var. *oreonastes* with dark green, very narrow leaves with thick rufous indumentum on the underside and neat little trusses with white or flushed rose flowers in April–May. Rather easier is *R. tsariense* with neat little leaves with semi-persistent indumentum on the upper surface and rufous indumentum on the lower surface. The pretty light pink flowers are spotted crimson. Another fine rufous indumented species is the long-lived *R. haematodes* with fleshy crimson-scarlet flowers in May–June. It needs a fairly open situation to flower well. For those that like flowers in shades of orange, *R. dichroanthum* and its subspecies are a must. These may eventually grow to 2m, but this will take many years. Their flowering season is similar to *R. haematodes*. Unfortunately all these are susceptible to root rot and it is advisable to plant them in soil that has never had rhododendrons in it before.

Now for dwarf lepidote hybrids. It seems that most hybridisers have totally neglected these apart from the late Warren Berg, a few hybridisers in eastern North America, one in Germany and ourselves. Why? Perhaps it is because few people grow enough dwarf species to be able to select the most promising parents or because most hybridisers prefer to produce the big blousy elepidote crosses. There is a great range of dwarf species to work with and we are convinced that there is still a great amount of successful hybridising to do here. If climate change is really upon us, we must breed for the future. To us one species stands out as a parent. It appears to be tough enough to give its progeny sufficient hardiness for most British gardens and it is epiphytic in the wild, thus drought resistant. Only introduced in the 1980s, it has become moderately well-known in the last ten years, James Cullen does not even mention it in his recent book *Hardy Rhododendron Species*, but it is already showing promise as a parent. This is *R. dendrocharis* (see below), a close relative of the less hardy, larger and earlier flowering *R. moupinense*, itself a great late winter flowerer with beautiful pink or white moderately frost-resistant flowers. *R.* 'Plover' is our best *R. dendrocharis* hybrid to date, crossed with the tender *R. edgeworthii* with deep pink scented flowers in April–May. A good hybrid of the latter is *R.* 'Tinkerbird' with large pale pink scented flowers with hairy leaves which grows to under a metre.

When we started hybridising dwarfs, the only ones of note were the 'blues' and the first of these are now superseded, such as *R.* 'Blue Diamond'. Our favourites are *R.* 'Penheale Blue' growing to 1m with deep violet blue flowers; *R.* 'Night Sky' to 60cm with lighter shade; and *R.* 'Sacko' shorter still, again with deep purple-blue flowers, all in April–May. *R.* 'Ramapo' can be added with its fine grey blue-green foliage and pale violet flowers. *R.* 'Frosthexe' is a newcomer from Germany with strong violet flowers with a reddish tinged base.

Yellows have been amongst our favourites from the start, using the parents *R. ludlowii, R. fletcherianum* and *R. keiskei* 'Yaku Fairy' plus others. One of our early crosses, *R.* 'Curlew' still has to be considered the best, if it gets away with not being frosted in the bud. Its flowers are large, its foliage healthy. *R.* 'Peter Bee' is a new one of Warren Berg's who kindly named it for the co-author. It is more upright but compact, very easy and floriferous, The well-known *R.* 'Patty Bee' is another Berg cross with large pale yellow flowers. Another of our hybrids which is rather different is *R.* 'Merganser' with yellow bell-shaped *R. campylogynum*-like flowers contrasting with dark green leaves, glaucous beneath. *R.* 'Wren' is the smallest, forming a tight mat. All flower in April and May.

There are pinks that may be just too pink for some people including our own excellent pink *R.* 'Pintail' (see facing page). You will notice many of

PETER COX

Rhododendron dendrocharis

the hybrids mentioned are named after birds and this is because we like birds as much as we like rhododendrons. *R.* 'Brambling' is perhaps even better, bright pink, a strong healthy grower with pink flowers on a low tight bush. With most unusual long lasting upright tubular flowers, *R.* 'Razorbill' adds variety. All flower in April–May. Earlier is the old favourite *R.* 'Cilpinense' which people scorn for regularly getting frosted but if placed under the shelter of a tree often gets away with flowering to perfection with its large showy pale and deeper pink flowers. Another early is the hot pink *R.* 'Tessa Roza' which may need occasional pruning to avoid straggliness. Very hardy from eastern USA is *R.* 'Weston's Pink Diamond' with semi-double fuchsia-pink flowers on a vigorous semi-deciduous bush.

Whites give a good contrast to the colours but few other hybridisers seem to have had much interest in them. One of the first we raised was *R.* 'Ptarmigan' and it is still popular. Although it often starts to open its flowers in March, it is rarely all frosted at once, so a second flush can come in April. It grows wider than tall. A little taller, to 60cm is *R.* 'Egret'. This is really different from all the others with masses of little creamy white bells like fairy thimbles. Slightly taller again is the prolific *R.* 'Crane' which is very easy to grow. The tough North American *R.* 'Dora Amateis' with its larger leaves, has very freely produced white flowers with a pale pink flush. A newer, early flowering cross raised in eastern Canada, so very hardy, is *R.* 'Isola Bella' with quite large palest pink flowers fading to white. Even earlier is *R.* 'Lucy Lou' with large pure white flowers with dark stamens on a rounded bush. This will perform best with some overhead protection.

Reds are scarce in lepidote dwarfs as there are few parent species to work with. Two of our most promising have gone down with rust fungus and leaf spot. Rust in particular has been responsible for the scrapping of several promising hybrids over the years and is hard to control. The nearest we have to red at the moment is *R.* 'Quail'. Low and compact, it has bright red buds which open to deep reddish pink.

There are now several bi-colours available which add to the colour range. *R.* 'Strawberry

PETER COX

Rhododendron 'Pintail'

Cream' forms an upright but tidy bush with shiny leaves. The flowers are yellowish-pink, striped deeper outside and its sister *R.* 'Barnaby Sunset' has pale yellow flowers, pink on the reverse. *R.* 'Tree Creeper' is one of our newest selections with flowers pink on the outside, cream within. *R.* 'Wee Bee' is another Berg introduction and one of the best dwarf hybrids ever raised, with frilled two-tone pale and deep pink flowers on a low tight bush. Perhaps the best-known Berg hybrid is *R.* 'Ginny Gee' which smothers itself in white flushed pink flowers, again low and tight.

A good selection of dwarf species can add more variety in both flower and foliage and length of the flowering season than the hybrids. To start the flowering in warmer sheltered gardens, *R. leucaspis*, with its almost round hairy leaves and flat white flowers contrasting with dark anthers, flowers in March–April. It makes a rounded bush of under one metre. Very different are the hardy twiggy Lapponicas with smaller leaves and flowers. To one metre is *R. hippophaeoides* 'Haba Shan' with deep powder-blue flowers that will tolerate several degrees of frost in April–May. Lower with fine glaucous foliage and blue purple flowers is *R. fastigiatum* of which the best is a selection from CH 7159. Different again is section Pogonanthum with aromatic foliage and little daphne-like flowers. A charmer is the dwarf *R. anthopogon* subsp. *hypenanthum* 'Annapurna' with pale yellow flowers in April–May. Taller, to 60cm and very free flowering is *R. primuliflorum* 'Doker La' with clear pink flowers while a little later is *R. trichostomum*, again with pink flowers.

R. campylogynum is one of our favourites, a little tricky to grow well but worth the trouble. There are several different forms but all have nodding little campanulate flowers which vary in colour from cream through pink, to claret and red with very neat little leaves, often dark and shiny. These flower in May–June. Subsection Saluenensia gives us some of the finest dwarf species. The glaucous, small-leaved *R. calostrotum* 'Gigha' covers itself with large rosy-red flowers in May. Later in May-June is the almost prostrate *R. calostrotum* subsp. *keleticum,* and its relative Radicans Group with even smaller leaves. These have flat-faced purple flowers held on stalks above the leaves. A little taller and even later flowering is *R. calostrotum* subsp. *riparium* Nitens Group with deep purplish pink flowers in June–July.

Last but not least is *R. lepidostylum* with the best glaucous leaves of any dwarf and late yellow flowers in June–July. This remains low to 60cm or a little more, but can get to a metre or more across where happy. It prefers light soil with a free root run.

To give another extension to the flowering period, evergreen azaleas containing *R. nakaharai* give us excellent ground cover and bright colours around and after mid-summer. *R.* 'Wombat' makes a pink carpet in late May, *R.* 'Squirrel' bright scarlet in May–June and *R.* 'Racoon' rounds off the season in June–July with masses of bright red flowers. All bred at Glendoick, you now know we also like mammals!

Peter Cox, well known as a leading authority on rhododendrons, and with his father, creator of the famous nursery at Glendoick in 1953, has made over 20 plant-hunting expeditions and is the author of many books on rhododendrons. His wife Patricia founded Glendoick Garden Centre in 1973, and later designed its Pagoda Garden

The Goddess Magnolia – EH Wilson's Finest Introduction?

Jim Gardiner

Ernest Wilson is one of the best known of all plant collectors who travelled primarily to China during the latter part of the 19th and early 20th centuries. Initially this was for the firm of Messrs. Veitch & Co., and then for the Arnold Arboretum. When examining the woody plant contents of gardens today, it is quite likely you will be able to find plants whose origins can be traced back to being a Wilson introduction.

He made four collecting trips to western China between 1899 and 1911, concentrating on the provinces of Hubei and Sichuan. He followed in the footsteps of the French missionary-zoologist Père Jean Pierre Armand David and of Augustine Henry, an Irishman who was an officer of the Chinese Imperial Maritime Customs Service. All of them would have travelled to the interior of China via the Yangtze river to the first of the famous limestone gorges. It was at the port of Yichang where they would have disembarked before moving into the foothills and mountain ranges where they made their discoveries.

Wilson is credited with introducing more magnolias into cultivation than anyone else – *Magnolia dawsoniana*, *M. delavayi*, *M. officinalis*, *M. sargentiana*, *M. sinensis*, *M. sprengeri* and *M. wilsonii*. Despite this, it is ironic that Wilson wrote comparatively little about the genus. He published two articles, the first in the *Gardeners' Chronicle* of 1906 (Vol.39, 3rd series) and a chapter in *Aristocrats of the Trees* (1930), while a previously unpublished article appeared in the *Journal of the Magnolia Society International* (formerly the American Magnolia Society) in 1980 (Vol 16.2):

JIM GARDINER

Magnolia sprengeri var. *elongata*

'In the parts of China I have travelled in, magnolias are nowhere really common plants. Locally, here and there, individuals are fairly plentiful but numerically they constitute an infinitesimal percentage of the forest flora. They occur in thickets, woodlands and mixed forests where the soil is cool, deep and rich in humus. Often they grow alongside streams or ponds. M. wilsonii *and its relatives frequently grow in rocky places, especially by streams, but always where a woodland soil obtains. In blossom they are, of course, among the most conspicuous, but in the half light of the forest, over hanging still reaches or rushing waters of a mountain torrent, the white saucer-shaped, crimson anthered blossoms of* M. wilsonii *make a delightful picture.'*

He owes his success to the methods he used to transport Magnolia seed:

'In later years I found by not removing the scarlet jacket and by wrapping each seed separately in waxed paper that the seeds would travel in paper packets through the mail.'

However, the scope of this article is to discuss *Magnolia sprengeri* var. *sprengeri* 'Diva' (see above), arguably his finest woody plant introduction and not to cover all the magnolias he introduced.

During Wilson's first Veitch expedition, he was collecting in western Hubei in the vicinity of Yichang. Reading his entry in *Plantae Wilsonianae*, vol 1 (pp. 401–402): Western Hubei: Changyang Hsien, moist woods, 6 April 1900 and September 1901 (Veitch Exped. Nos 21, 21a and seed No. 688), he described this as *M. denudata* var. *purpurascens* and continued throughout his life to use this name. So, in 1930, in *Aristocrats of the Trees*, he wrote:

'I shall ever remember my first sight of this magnolia. It was a fine specimen fully 60 feet tall, with a broad, more or less pyramidal crown and was laden with thousands of fully expanded blossoms. Never again did I see such a magnificent example of this magnolia illuminating the woodland landscapes of China.'

JIM GARDINER

Magnolia sprengeri var. *sprengeri* 'Diva'

Why Wilson was so adamant in maintaining this name, when *M. denudata* has nine tepals whereas *M. sprengeri* has twelve, is a mystery.

Before dealing with the plant itself, I shall briefly cover the background botany. In preparing the text for *Curtis's Botanical Magazine* 9116 in 1926, Dr Otto Stapf noted:

'Mr J.E. Dandy... called my attention to Pampanini's M. sprengeri, *the originals of which had just been received at Kew on loan from Florence. These consisting of some branches with flower buds and a few open flowers but without leaves, had been collected by the Italian missionary*

JIM GARDINER

Magnolia sprengeri 'Copeland Court'

PC Silvestri in Northern Hupeh in 1912 and 1913. They match so completely with specimens of Wilson's M. denudata *var.* purpurascens, *that Mr. Dandy and I have come to the conclusion that the two sets are conspecific.'*

Returning to the plant, seedlings of W.688 were raised at Veitch's Coombe Wood Nursery during the winter/spring of 1901/ 02 and presumably were eventually lined out. When Sir Harry Veitch retired from the business in 1913, the company held a great sale of plants. As the batch labelled W.688 had not flowered, they were auctioned off and bought by JC Williams, the Lord Aberconway and RBG Kew. We know for certain that three plants went to Kew, two to Bodnant and one to Caerhays. At Kew, WJ Bean noted that all three trees had white flowers with a slight purple stain at the base, similarly at Bodnant. In GH Johnstone's *Asiatic Magnolias in Cultivation*, published in 1955, he noted that both the Kew and Bodnant trees had developed into upright growing small trees of a close bushy habit varying between 20 and 30 feet in height. These flowered for the first time at Kew in 1926, in excess of 20 years from germination. Wilson regarded the white flowered form as *M. denudata* var. *elongata* which Stapf confirmed in *Curtis's Botanical Magazine* as *M. sprengeri* var. *elongata* (see p.38).

The Caerhays plant was placed by JC Williams in a new area of the garden and, much to his surprise, flowered on the 20 April 1919, approximately 17 years from germination. Instead of white flowers it bloomed with beautiful rose pink flowers. Even before it flowered, it was far more vigorous than the other five. But when it flowered, the tepals had greater substance and were beautifully presented, being an attractive cup before fully opening to a

JOHN GALLAGHER

Magnolia sprengeri 'Eric Savill'

JOHN GALLAGHER

Magnolia sprengeri 'Eric Savill'

saucer shape, rich rose pink on the outside, white suffused with pink on the inside. If there was any hint of either the pink or white forms to be of hybrid origin, this can be more or less discounted because of the time taken for each to flower for the first time. If this plant was a hybrid, then I would have expected it to flower within ten years.

It is strange that only one rose pink flowered plant was raised from this batch, while five with white flowers were produced. Wilson regarded the white form 'as rare in the wild, and most usually met with rosy or reddish pink flowers.'

Wei-Bang Sun of Kunming Botanical Garden tells me that 'the white flowered form is not common in natural habitats' and that in China both the white and pink flowered forms are regarded as *M. sprengeri*. It is commonly known as Wu-Dang and Hu-Bei mulan, the 'harbinger of spring' (Ying-Chun-Shu).

It appears to me that if the Chinese collectors knew the white and pink flowered forms as the same, then they must have combined any seed lots collected from different sources under the one collector's number, hence both appearing under W.688.

The tree that Wilson described so glowingly in *Aristocrats of the Trees* must have been the mother of the Caerhays 'Diva', probably growing by a roadside, or beside a temple. Augustine Henry and others who travelled the short distance from the river port of Yichang south to the district of Changyang must have known this tree, as Wilson credited Henry with making the first collection of this in 1888.

A little over 100 years on from the original introduction of seed into this country, what makes this plant so special?

Each year during March and April, all magnolia growers wait with bated breath to see

Magnolia sprengeri 'Wakehurst'

Magnolia sprengeri 'Marwood Spring'

if there will be a frost the following morning. Despite flowering from mid- March onwards through April, rarely will you find the quality of the flowers impaired, unlike other tree magnolias. Not only is the flower resilient, so is the plant's hardiness rating regarded so highly, particularly by the Americans. The late Phil Savage Jr, a former President of the Magnolia Society International, gardened at Bloomfield Hills Michigan where temperatures can fall as low as –34°C (–29°F), Zone 6. He saw the value of *M. sprengeri* as a seed parent as he considered that the geographic range of *M. sprengeri* extended to the north of its point of collection in Hubei. Joseph Hers, a Belgian who was General Secretary of the General Company of Chinese Railways and Tramways, collected to the north of Hubei in Henan Province. In the early 1920s he collected herbarium specimens of magnolias and sent them to the Arnold Arboretum which were identified as *M. denudata* var. *purpurascens*. Savage believed that Hers's specimens were *M. sprengeri,* making it the most northerly species of this group of Yulania. In many respects Savage's forecast was correct. As well as the species itself being hardy in Michigan, its progeny have turned out to be even hardier.

So we have a plant that is straight-forward to cultivate and that flowers reliably and continuously over several weeks in March and April. It also sets good seed; indeed the seedpods themselves are spectacular, weighing down branches to the point of breaking. It hybridises with a wide range of species and hybrids, often with spectacular success. The US National Arboretum hybrids of 'Galaxy' and 'Spectrum' (with *M. liliiflora*) and more recently with *M. sargentiana* var. *robusta* at Caerhays to produce 'J.C. Williams' are particularly fine examples.

Having an abundance of fine flowers is for nought if the habit of the plant is poor. However, *M. sprengeri* produces a beautifully symmetrical tree which can vary from a medium sized crown to one that is large and upright to 80ft in height.

Throughout British gardens a fine array of named first or second generation seedlings of *M. sprengeri* var. *sprengeri* 'Diva' have arisen. They vary in size and colour from rose purple, rose pink or clear pink on the outside

JOHN GALLAGHER

Magnolia sprengeri 'Burncoose'

PHILIP EVANS

Magnolia sprengeri 'Lanhydrock'

to pale pink fading to white on the inside. At Wisley, the finest is 'Copeland Court' (see p.40) with its 8 inch rich clear pink flowers. However, at Marwood Hill, the garden in north Devon of Dr Jimmy Smart, 'Marwood Spring' (see p.42) catches the eye. It was John Bond who named a Caerhays seedling of *M. sprengeri* after Eric Savill (see pp40–41) while the tallest clone of *M. sprengeri* by far is at Westonbirt Arboretum, which when I saw it last was about 80 feet. The Cornish gardens of Burncoose, Antony, Lanhydrock and Lamellen, Bodnant in north Wales ('Claret Cup') and the Royal Botanic Gardens at Wakehurst Place all have excellent examples which never fail to impress.

Sadly, the original introduction at Caerhays is no longer with us, although I understand that the true 'Diva' lives on, as the master propagator Otto Eisenhut has grafted from the Caerhays tree. However, its progeny can be found in most countries around the world where magnolias are growing, a tribute indeed to that remarkable plant that JC Willams bought at that famous Coombe Wood sale nearly 100 years ago.

References

BEAN, WJ Magnolias-Chinese species. *The New Flora and Silva* Vol 5:1 (1932)
Curtis's Botanical Magazine Tab.9116 (1926)
Gardeners' Chronicle Vol 39 3rd series (1906)
GARDINER, JM *Magnolias: A Gardener's Guide* (2000)
HUNT, D *Magnolias and their allies* (1998)
JOHNSTONE, GH *Asiatic Magnolias in Cultivation* (1955)
LANCASTER, R *Travels in China* (1989)
Magnolia: Journal of the Magnolia Society International Vol 16:2 (1980)
MILLAIS, JG *Magnolias* (1927)
WILLIAMS, J The origins and developments of magnolias at Caerhays. *The Cornish Garden*
WILSON, EH *Plantae Wilsonianae Vol 1* Edited by CS Sargent (1913)

Jim Gardiner is Curator of RHS Garden Wisley, and a former President of the Magnolia Society International. A leading expert on magnolias, he is author of the book Magnolias: A Gardener's Guide

Rhododendron densifolium – A Mainland Vireya in Cultivation

George Argent

LYNSEY MUIR

Rhododendron densifolium

Rhododendron densifolium KM Feng (section Pseudovireya) is one of the small flowered mainland species with bright starry yellow flowers similar to the better known and long cultivated *R. vaccinioides* Hook f. which differs in having white or pale pinkish flowers. It is also similar to the much larger *R. emarginatum* Hemsl. & EH Wilson and some of the other yellow-flowered mainland pseudo-vireyas, but it has consistently smaller leaves than these plants – *R. densifolium* leaves rarely exceeding 5mm in width. The flowers of *R. densifolium* are of a clear yellow (*RHS Colour Chart* 11A) and without conspicuous spots on the upper lobes which the forms of *R. emarginatum* always seem to have in cultivation.

Rhododendron densifolium flowered for the first time in cultivation in the garden of Eric Annal on 6 October 2006, from wild plants collected from a limestone hill in Yunnan province, China by Ms G Bailey. Mr Annal's plant is, as yet, only 20cm high although descriptions from the wild suggest it may grow up to 1.3m. Personal observations of this species are that it is more usually mat forming, growing semi-prostrate and rooting along its branches in loose moss under light shade.

An interesting feature of Mr Annal's plant is that the ovary is densely scaly but does not have hairs as described, although in all other respects this plant conforms to the description of *R. densifolium* (Feng 1983). This raises the possibility that it may be a distinct variety or subspecies, as the indumentum on the ovary has been considered an important character in species delimitation in this group. Unfortunately we have little information on the variability of this species in the wild. The individual flowers do not appear to last very long, remaining open for about a week, but the spreading to revolute lobes and protruding brown anthers have a dainty charm. Mr Annal's plant has so far produced six flowers over a period of about three weeks.

R. densifolium is unlikely to become a horticulturally important plant as its appeal will be more to those who like cultivating species but its foliage alone makes it more attractive than most of the other rhododendrons in Pseudovireya with the exception of the elegant blue-green foliage of *R. rushforthii* Argent & DF Chamb.

Mr Annal's plant has been cultivated under the usual 'vireya' conditions in an open acid compost and been grown in a cool glasshouse with humidity maintained at between 85% and 90% and given frost protection. It is recorded in the wild growing up to 1800m in altitude, much lower than most of the other pseudovireyas. This means it is unlikely to be as hardy as has been claimed for some of the other species in this section. *R. rushforthii* is said to have withstood temperatures down to –8°C (Argent 2006) and *R. kawakamii* Hayata has been grown outdoors in Edinburgh in a sheltered position for the last eight winters (Paul Smith *pers. comm.*).

Although probably needing frost protection in Britain it is hoped that this species will become more widely grown.

Acknowledgements
With thanks to Eric Annal for bringing this plant to my attention and for many helpful discussions about this species. Thanks also to Lynsey Muir for the photographs.

References

ARGENT G, 2006. *Rhododendrons of Subgenus Vireya*. The Royal Horticultural Society, London, 1-382.

FENG KM, 1983. New Species and Varieties of Rhododendron from Yunnan. *Acta Botanica Yunnan* 5: 3, 265-270.

George Argent is a research associate at the Royal Botanic Garden Edinburgh having retired from his position as tropical botanist in 2004. He has worked for the last 30 years on SE Asian plants, especially rhododendrons and bananas. He has previously worked in Brazil and West Africa

Darts Hill Garden Park – A Plantsman's Garden in British Columbia

Graham Laine

From land that was first logged just 50 or 60 years beforehand, Darts Hill Garden Park was begun in the 1940s by Francisca and Edwin Darts as a rural getaway. It is located in the Fraser River valley south of Vancouver, British Columbia, Canada in what is now the City of Surrey, close by the US border. One can see salt water to the southwest and 3285m-high volcano Mount Baker to the southeast. The south-facing slope of the seven-and-a-half acres is an ideal exposure for most of our ornamental plants.

In the beginning, massive stumps and mountains of wood debris had to be removed. After the house was built in 1947, a mixed orchard was planted. Little remains of the orchard now, long since replaced by ornamental trees and shrubs – notably magnolias and rhododendrons. These soon produced a garden of great interest throughout the year and one of spectacular colour during the extended coastal spring of the Pacific Northwest.

The Darts were passionate collectors of both the best performers and the newest introductions to the area. They were regular callers upon nurserymen such as the Gosslers of Gossler Farm Nursery in Eugene, Oregon. Both Francisca and Ed were very active in Vancouver horticultural organisations and received much material through these associations. Today, the garden has a great diversity of woody and herbaceous plants ranging from the ordinary to the unusual to the latest collections from Asia and South America. Francisca will be 90 in 2006, and is still testing the limits of hardiness as she continues to add to her garden.

As one walks up the drive towards the house, plants of the 1940s and 1950s predominate. Here in the remnants of the orchard are *Abies pinsapo*, *Calocedrus decurrens*, *Magnolia* × *soulangeana*, *Corylus avellana* 'Contorta', *Parrotia persica*, *Mespilus germanica*, *Hamamelis mollis*, and closer to the house a 60-foot *Picea orientalis* with *Wisteria floribunda* growing to the top.

Just below the house is a magnificent walnut cross of the Eastern American Butternut and the Japanese Walnut, *Juglans cinerea* × *J. ailanthifolia* var. *cordiformis*. This tree is beautiful from any angle in any season.

Continuing on down through mature rhododendron plantings into mixed shrub beds with many pieris varieties, there is a higher canopy of well-spaced trees. Many of these are large magnolias including *Magnolia macrophylla*, *M. salicifolia*,

Darts Hill Garden: view with *Magnolia* 'Merrill' and *Magnolia* 'Wada's Memory'

M. kobus, M. acuminata, M. cordata and *M. tripetala.*

A small grass field remains below the house that is bordered on two sides by a new 'Magnolia Walk' with at least forty varieties. In addition to the old standbys, there are many new hybrids as well as some new species collections. Species such as *Magnolia fraseri, M. microphylla* var. *ashei* and *M. officinalis* and several of the former *Michelias* are here. *M. maudiae* flowered for the first time this year, in a new, better protected location.

Winter-flowering shrubs are an important part of this garden. *Hamamelis mollis, Chimonanthus praecox, Lonicera purpusii* and *Azara microphylla* fill the garden with scent during the typical overcast days of our wet winters.

Moving into spring, of the many points of interest in the garden, one of the best in mid-April is a long path, walled on each side by many forms of *Rhododendron augustinii.*

Of all the scented plants in the garden, my favorite is *Magnolia* × *thompsoniana* – a fine, small tree of low spreading habit producing a continuous display of gorgeously scented white flowers. These are within easy reach and bloom over a long summer period. No fragrant garden is complete without *Philadelphus* × *purpureomaculatus* 'Belle Etoile'. Ours grows in full sun.

Some other trees and shrubs of particular interest include *Nothofagus antarctica*, appearing like a giant bonsai above a stone wall; a majestic *Abies nordmanniana* with deep-green foliage contrasting well with surrounding plants; and the deciduous

CHARLES SALE

Darts Hill Garden: view with *Magnolia 'Elizabeth'* and *Ponciris trifoliata*

swamp cypress from the southern US, *Taxodium distichum.* It is well sited to show its many root nodules (knees) in a damp position below a pond.

Above the pond a huge *Ulmus parvifolia* (Chinese Elm) leans out from the edge of the forest and towers over mature 20-foot rhododendrons. Also close to the pond, two large *Malus hupehensis* fill the air with their scent on a calm warm day in early May.

A few prickly shrubs should be mentioned: the attractive (but don't get too close) Chilean *Colletia hystrix* 'Rosea' with masses of tiny pink flowers in late summer; and also in late summer the small yellowish green flowers of *Paliurus spina-christi.* In spring, the white *Rosa sericea* subsp. *omeiensis* f. *pteracantha* is a species rose of great character.

In 1994, the year that Ed died, the garden was donated to the City of Surrey. Francisca still lives at her garden and plays a large role in its management. Following the gift, a task force was formed to set up the Darts Hill Garden Conservancy Trust Society. It is now in place and through an operating agreement assists the city in managing the garden.

Why not come to the beautiful Pacific West Coast and our garden this spring?

Graham Laine is the Head Gardener at Darts Hill Garden Park

From Sherwood to Shillong – A Plant Journey in Northeast India

Vaughan Gallavan

In October 2004, I joined Alan Clark and Jane Brazendale on an expedition to Arunachal Pradesh and Nagaland, in North Eastern India. This was to be my first taste of plant hunting.

Alan, a veteran of some sixteen previous expeditions, had initially invited me to go to China – a plan that was abandoned with uncertainties over the SARS virus. Instead, it was decided to follow in the footsteps of Peter Cox's group, who had visited Arunachal Pradesh in the spring of 2004. In addition, we were to visit Mount Japfu in Nagaland.

Peter and Kenneth Cox have travelled extensively in Arunachal Pradesh and must be regarded as contemporary authorities on the region. Peter wrote an informative account of his expedition in the 2006 yearbook, through which I was able to relive some of my experience.

Although both of our groups covered the same ground and saw mostly the same plants, I will endeavour to avoid repetition. Peter Cox's group saw plenty of bloom and leeches but perhaps less of the general mountainscape. We saw few flowers but were blessed, for the most part, with clear conditions and not a leech in sight. Our itinerary was arranged and supported by the same team: Oken Tayeng, the tour manager; Katu Bage and Rajin Giri, our 'minders'; Tashi Phuntso Lubrang, Village Chief and local guide. All were most competent, attentive, kind and friendly. We also employed yak herdsmen and porters who were equally conscientious and good-humoured. These people were a delight to be with.

Our journey from Guwahati, the capital of Assam, to Dirang, our base town, was meant to be a 14-hour drive. The monsoon had ceased four days earlier but flooding was still widespread. A tributary of the great Brahmaputra had washed away a major road bridge, adding to our journey time. For miles we passed people who had been displaced by the floodwaters and had made temporary homes on roadside levees.

We crossed the border to Arunachal Pradesh and immediately began the steep ascent through pristine, warm temperate forest, screaming with cicadas. 'This is not a rally, please enjoy my valley' read the first of many quaint road safety advice signs. Quaint signs on the hair-raising, blind-cornered, helter-skeltering, yet most beautifully breath-taking stretches of road. *Luculia gratissima* in full, sweet scented, pink bloom was common here and one of the few plants we were to see in flower. These warm temperate forests and

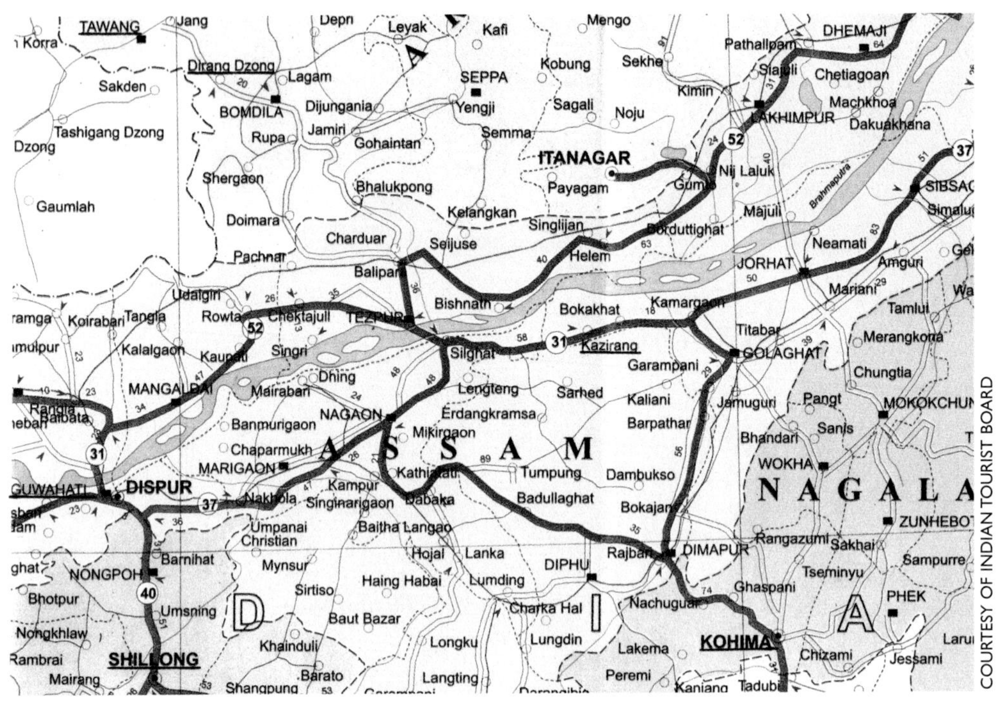

Regional map of the area of the journey (main roads in purple), showing Guwahati in Assam, the start point on the Brahmaputra (left-hand edge of map), with the Arunachal Pradesh/Bhutan border area to the immediate north. Bottom right is Kohima in Nagaland, and Shillong in Magalaya is bottom left.

their inhabitants remain a tantalizing mystery to me. With only a few exceptions, the plants were strangers.

We arrived in Dirang after dark and stayed in a government guesthouse attached to a yak research station. There was a morning of recuperation as our team prepared provisions for our first excursion towards the Poshing La. As with the spring group, we were taken by pickup truck to the village of Chander, ascending steep tracks through managed mixed woodland. This included *Pinus wallichiana* and *Rhododendron arboreum*, the latter coppiced for firewood. As we approached our base camp, at Chander, we exchanged greetings with a group of Monba people, laden with saws and faggots of timber. These villagers were our hosts for the night and some of them, our companions for the next six days. The temperature had plummeted and we wrapped up warm to explore the scrubland nearby. Here I made my first acquaintance with *Crawfurdia speciosa*, a climbing member of the gentian family, blooming spectacularly in the twilight. Other plants were more familiar, hypericum species, cotoneaster, gaultheria and berberis, one reminiscent of *Berberis insignis*, with large spinose leaves on spineless stems. Frank Kingdon Ward collected *Berberis dasyclada* (subsection Insignis) less than a day's walk from this location. We returned to supper and a warm Monba reception, exchanging songs and

Alan Clark and companions on the Poshing La

cautiously sipping at grubby mugs of *chang*, a rice wine, replenished after every sip.

Chander woke early to the sounds of children and livestock. Over the smoke-filtering bamboo roofs of the stone huts, we caught our first sight of distant, snow-clad peaks suspended above ridges of dense forest. Inside an hour, mountain and cloud were almost indistinguishable, like a thin veil floating over the forest. The clouds cast a leopard patchwork of green tones beneath the clear blue sky. Vegetation within a broad radius of the village was scrubby on account of grazing and firewood coppicing. Tall bamboo poles, dressed with long prayer flags, framed views over coniferous woodland to paddy fields in the valley bottoms. We thanked our hosts and left along a barely maintained military track. In the scrub were *Magnolia campbellii* and *R. kendrickii,* both having been coppiced at some stage. *R. edgeworthii* was growing on a damaged stool of a lithocarpus; hydrangeas and viburnums were in abundance, as were the fruits of arisaemas, nestling around tree roots.

After half an hour our support team passed us in a mellifluous jangle of yak bells and herdsmen's song. Whether nearby or in the distance, this 'music' was ever present, blending perfectly with nature's other sounds, exotic birds, cicadas and the cries of monkeys.

I was extremely grateful for Alan's company, as I was overwhelmed by a plant

VAUGHAN GALLAVAN

Tongri – dawn over Assam plains

identification crisis. Here were various plants that I work with every day, now somehow unfamiliar in their natural setting. My recognition of rhododendrons was limited. I had compiled a target list from the *Encyclopedia of Rhododendrons* by Peter and Kenneth Cox and had visited the relevant plants here, at Sherwood, where I am head gardener. I was therefore able to identify a few at first and, with Alan's help, several more over the following weeks. I was happy to spot the enormous buds of *R. lindleyi*, out of proportion to its spindly stems, sprawling over a rocky outcrop.

Saplings of *Betula utilis* were a regular find, their sunlit, peeling red bark mimicking prayer flags. Later, on our descent through warm temperate forest, we saw a fine mature specimen, over two feet in diameter and with its crown dressed in golden epiphytic ferns. Various climbers, including clematis, actinidia and holboellia, twined themselves through the trees below us. The track from Chander to Tongri had most likely been made in the 1960s, well after Frank Kingdon Ward's last visit in 1938. Its relatively gentle gradient was an advantage in our acclimatisation to the altitude of about 3000m although our progress was too slow to reach our target camp for the first day. We spent too much time 'stopping to gape at weeds' *(Frank Kingdon Ward – The Last of the Great Plant Hunters* by Charles Lyte, 1989, p.72).

The next day, in addition to small trees of *Schefflera impressa* and *Hydrangea heteromalla*, we came upon a *Magnolia campbellii*, with a glaucous under-leaf and purple twig growth – not like anything that I had seen before. My excitement grew as we approached the rhododendron forest topped by *Abies densa*, its blown-out crowns in the distance almost resembling *Araucaria araucana*. These giants

VAUGHAN GALLAVAN

Rhododendron hookeri tunnel

were dripping in epiphytic growth of mosses, lichens, vaccinicums, *R. megeratum* and even larger plants, apparently *R. leptocarpum*. Some fine old acers, possibly *campbellii*, were some of the last of the taller broadleaved trees in this transitional zone, though lithocarpus, quercus and other genera filled the valleys below.

At Tongri, I rose to watch the dawn, perhaps my most memorable experience of the trip. To the northeast, I saw Mount Gori Chen at 6488m, more than twice our altitude, pink in the first light and backed by yet higher peaks in Tibet. To the east, the skeletal crowns of *Abies densa* were silhouetted against progressively fading forested ridges, all the way to the plains of Assam. On my return from this expedition, I read *Assam Adventure* and found Kingdon Ward's photograph taken from almost the same viewpoint. For the next three days we walked along the same ridge that he had twice visited. The military track had ended at Tongri and we now followed a more undulating, rugged path, through some of the most magnificent natural vegetation that I have experienced, a jungle of garden-worthy plants.

Here, *Enkianthus deflexus*, *Daphne bholua* and *Magnolia globosa* were growing as the under-storey to *R. hookeri*, 40 feet tall. *R. argipeplum*, with its handsome red flaking bark and *R. falconeri* alongside *Sorbus macallisteri* – all, in turn, hosts to a variety of smaller plants. Not frequent, but very spectacular in its early autumnal tones, was a small sorbus with very fine leaflets. I imagine that this may have been *S. microphylla*.

The soil here was sandy and very free-draining, there were no post-monsoon puddles and our boots were rarely muddy. I found it interesting that these plants get plenty of rain through the summer months and have relatively dry conditions in winter – practically

VAUGHAN GALLAVAN

Lake near Bhutanese border

the opposite to the climate in Britain. Also, large-leaved rhododendrons were seen, thriving in full exposure to the sun and wind. Regrettably, as we reached higher alpine slopes, it began to snow and our guides thought it in our best interests to turn back. It was not such a hardship to backtrack as we saw more on the way down and had to camp once more at Tongri.

On the last day of this trek we made a rapid descent through warm temperate woodland. As we began the 600m scramble down, we saw *R. griffithianum* and *R. dalhousiae* var. *rhabdotum* and another member of Magnoliaceae. In the dense forest undergrowth were the tall fruiting spikes of hedychiums. *Primula geranifolia* covered shady wet banks and we were staggered by the enormity of *Alnus nepalensis*, looking more like poplars in dimension.

Oxygen levels rose, as did our spirits at the prospect of a shower, a meal and a bed at the Hotel Pemaling, back in Dirang.

Another day off and provisions were replenished and camping chairs repaired. These had been damaged by the *dzos* (yak hybrids) squeezing through gulleys on the first trek. Unfortunately we had to say goodbye to these fantastic beasts after the first trek, as on the next we were to be accompanied by ponies and new musical variations. Our drive to Naga GG, the next base camp, had been a mixed bag of excitement and despondency. We passed through some wonderful vegetation but then came to an area where acres of the forest had apparently been destroyed by fire. It seemed possible that the trees

VAUGHAN GALLAVAN

A hillside of Berberis and polygonum at Bangajang Gompa

had been deliberately killed for recent road building. To see the contrast between the pristine vegetation climax and this devastation was heart-breaking. Although the landscape did improve and we saw plenty of rhododendrons, our base camp felt a bleak place to alight, cold and wet underfoot. The water-meadow was frozen solid in the morning and we saw the frosted, over-wintering rosettes of the primulas that Peter Cox had described flowering in the spring.

We set out from camp and climbed steeply for much of the morning. Starting at over 3,000m, it was noticeably harder going than on the previous trek. Grand Firs were hung with very long strands of lichen through which we caught glimpses of the thawing campsite.

Most of the following six days were spent above the tree line, in a wonderful open landscape frequently dominated by *R. bhutanense*. We occasionally dipped back through forested valleys but otherwise steadily climbed towards the lake district of Bangajang. The nights grew progressively colder with a good fall of snow one morning. We were treated to dramatic colour contrasts. Autumn-red drifts of deciduous berberis emerged from the snow against a deep green forest backdrop. Rust coloured *R. anthopogon* and copper-tinged *Polygonum affine* covered steep slopes up to a clear blue skyline. Visibility was excellent, snow-peaked mountains just over the border in Bhutan were clear in detail as were the endless forested valleys in all directions but north, where the vegetation gave way to snow and rock.

My lingering memories of this part of the trip include beautiful lakes, gentians flowering through shallow snow, the golden-green rosettes of *Meconopsis paniculata*, the taste of yak cheese and the gentle fluttering sound of prayer flags in the breeze.

'Better Mr Late than a late mister' was another road sign, this time en-route to Tawang, birthplace of the sixth Dalai Lama. Here, in the largest Buddhist monastery in India, all the colours of the mountain scenery were reflected in the intricate and lavish decoration of the interior. 'Safety on the road means safe tea at home.' I hoped that our driver was taking notice of the signs while playing with his mobile phone.

After another night in Dirang we began the journey through the mountains to the plains of Assam. *Prunus cerasoides* was a highlight in the early stages of the long days drive. Three days had been spent in transit since our trek near the Bhutan border and although we had become more accustomed to the ways of the road, driving after dark was exhausting.

Set in a garden of some 240 well-labelled species of trees, shrubs and climbers, the Wild Grass Hotel at Kaziranga could not have been a better place for a tired plant-hunting team to break a journey. Surrounded by a cool green sea of tea, acacia and peppercorn vines, the hotel was only a short distance from the Kaziranga National Park. At dawn, we rode elephants through boggy areas of tall elephant grass. We saw the endangered one horned rhinoceros, water buffalo and various species of deer and many different birds. Taking a second excursion at dusk, wild elephants grazed nearby as we watched the sunset over the distant Himalayan range. Alas, we saw no tigers, only paw prints and the sparse remains of prey.

Kohima, the capital of Nagaland, was our next destination and another day of driving. Climbing Mount Japfu (Japvo) to see *R. macabeanum* was our main reason for the visit here. A team of six porters helped us on this relatively easy two-day trek. These young men were all students, more Western than their Himalayan counterparts, but a helpful and friendly bunch. It was very hot on the first leg of the trek, with a few miles of steady climbing through slash-and-burn farmland. *Pyrus pashia*, grown for fodder, fuel and fruit, had either been spared in the clearing process or had been introduced. Large yellow flowers, with a purple centre, were those of *Abelmoschus manihot*, an attractive plant, which was grown for its nutritious leaves and is related to okra. Buddlejas were widespread and varied with some good forms, one in particular similar to *B. forrestii*. As our single-track path neared the forest edge, we stepped aside to allow a young Naga man to pass. He was dragging four substantial wooden

VAUGHAN GALLAVAN

Mount Japfu (Japvo) – home of *Rhododendron macabeanum*

posts, attached to a thick strap which he wore over his head. Arriving under the forest canopy the path gradient steepened dramatically. We had to scramble straight up, several hundred metres of very loose soil, clinging to anything to avoid sliding back down. This was obviously a timber extraction route. I nearly missed seeing a huge michelia, I was so intent on staying on my feet. Soon after, we arrived at the overnight stop, a rough timber building with a veranda and one long sleeping platform. I dumped my bags and went to explore and to record the sounds of the forest. The broad-leaved evergreen cover was magnificent and as far as I know consisted mainly of quercus, lithocarpus and castanopsis. Acorns periodically cracked and crashed their way through the canopy to the ground with resounding thuds. A hard hat might have been advisable. I found a huge wooden frame that was used for converting timber on site, a technique not unlike pit sawing.

The remaining climb started as we had left off, steep and on loose soil but the paths were thankfully more meandering. We reached the ridge and found our first rhododendron, *R. elliottii.* This had been discovered by Sir George Watt in 1882 and introduced by Frank Kingdon Ward in 1927 and 1949. A small tree resembling sorbus, but with single-seeded red fruits, turned out to be a zanthoxylum sp. Ascending the ridge, we soon found *R. macabeanum,* frequently over 40 feet high, sometimes growing horizontally from the mountainside, pale indumentum under dark green ovate leaves. Much as I enjoyed seeing these plants, I found it hard to imagine where they might best be viewed when in flower. Beneath their canopy we saw, *R. johnstoneanum, R. manipurense*, skimmia, pieris, viburnum and phlomis. Close to the summit a stunted macabeanum was amidst *R. bauhiniiflorum*, *Buddleja candida* and a dwarf bamboo, harvested by the locals for making brushes. A metal-covered wooden cross marked the summit, but the expected views of rice-terraced hills towards Manipur were lost in cloud.

We managed the descent on the same day, the Hotel Japfu being more enticing than the smoky wooden hut on the mountain. The British High Commissioner to India, Sir Michael Arthur, and his deputy were also guests at the hotel. They had come to lay wreaths at the Kohima War Cemetery in tribute to those who had died in the battle there 60 years ago.

Our visit to this immaculately maintained memorial was a moving end to our stay in Nagaland. We spent three more days getting back to Guwahati making a detour via Shillong, the capital of Megalaya. Despite seeing some interesting plants, the managed landscape here was an anticlimax after the unspoilt forest of the mountains.

Since our return I have been absorbed in sourcing information on what we saw and experienced. I've been hungry for new books especially those on plant hunting. I've spent hours retracing our steps on Google Earth as no large-scale maps have been available. My interest in plants has taken a new turn as I find myself at the beginning of a steep, Himalayan learning curve. I am extremely grateful to those who have helped with and taken an interest in this trip.

Vaughan Gallavan is a member of the Southwest Branch of the Group. Since 1981 he has been Head Gardener at Sherwood, the Devon garden owned by Sir John and Lady Quicke. He also runs a small nursery at Sherwood Cottage, Newton St Cyres, Exeter specialising in magnolias, deciduous azaleas and other woody plants

Discovering the Azaleas of Southeast USA

Kevin Hughes

My first gardening job some 25 years ago was to tackle a 15-acre garden on ancient New Forest land that had fallen into chaos. The primary problem was a sea of the dread *Rhododendron ponticum* that was drowning the garden and native woodland alike. I can well remember the corpses of ancient fallen trees now submerged without trace, before any chance of regeneration could occur, beneath the so-called 'wild rhododendron'.

My training at that time was primarily in ecology, and professional gardening was a new venture for me. Until this point I had little or no knowledge of rhododendrons and that was coloured by a hatred of the invading weed *R. ponticum*. Growing at the base of a large *Sequoiadendron giganteum* was a rather straggly deciduous azalea. Unlike the yellow flowered *R. luteum* that also survived in this garden, this one had cream and pink flowers that would not have been out of place on a honeysuckle, and, importantly to me, it clearly was not an invader. I was and am keen on self-sustaining gardens, so I prefer plants that, once established, need no supplementary water. This azalea was growing on gravelly soil in the roots of a large conifer so perhaps it did not need the moist well-drained peaty soil so often mentioned in connection with this genus. Indeed, once the competing brambles and *R. ponticum* had been cleared away, combined with a little pruning, the azalea thickened up into a dense, floriferous bush. It was of course *R. periclymenoides*. Already addicted to trilliums, the journey of discovery that the identification of this azalea took me upon brought me to a 'road to Damascus' conversion that would change my whole view of the genus and lead me to a passion for the American flora, trilliums, magnolias and deciduous azaleas in particular.

I soon ran into difficulties when attempting to obtain the species I had read about: there was then no *RHS Plant Finder* or internet to help. Worse than the scarcity of these plants were discouraging comments from gardeners who suggested that American azaleas did not thrive in our gardens. I was able to track down some, *R. occidentale* and *R. atlanticum* being the first two, and these did just fine. In the years following I have been able to obtain most of the species and trial them in my own and clients' gardens and I can now honestly recommend them as very rewarding and, in many cases, highly adaptable shrubs for the garden.

In the wild, individual species occur in a wide range of habitats, typically on forest edges or on mountain balds, and the environment in which they grow has a huge impact on their habit. Not surprisingly those out in the open are often of lower stature and more compact than their cousins down in the forest. Sometimes these differences remain constant in gardens e.g. *R. viscosum* var. *montanum* will maintain the dwarf habit it possesses in its native Blue Ridge Mountains, but more often the plants will adjust accordingly when brought into gardens. So in the garden environment it is down to us, whether our chosen plants become drawn and straggly or compact and floriferous.

American gardeners will oft talk of placing their azaleas in shade, notably the late blooming *R. prunifolium* and it is perhaps in following that advice we in Britain sometimes go astray. We ought to remember that our sunshine strength is rather different to that of the southeast USA, where the sun shines in a manner akin to that of the Mediterranean or North Africa. Small wonder then azalea flowers can fry in their summer sun. Even assuming the UK climate is hotting up, it is unlikely ever to match that of the south east USA, so a shady site here can result in straggly, poor flowering plants. In my experience at least half a day exposed to full sun provides the best results and in full sun they can become outstanding specimens. This certainly works for *R. prunifolium* providing it receives adequate moisture at the roots in the summer.

In the wild, colonies of azaleas have often benefited from forestry operations which open up the canopy and allow in more light.

American azaleas can be divided into two subseries, Luteum and Canadense. In the latter only *R. vaseyi* occurs in the south east region. Known as the 'Pinkshell Azalea' it is a very localised plant in the wild where it is known only from a restricted area in North Carolina at elevations mostly above 1500m. Here it is best looked for in swamps and along steep wooded ravines. Fragmentation of its habitat, through development and the drainage of swamps, represent the greatest threat to the species in the wild. In its natural environment it can become a 4m plus shrub drawn up under the canopy of trees but 2m would be more normal in gardens. Flat-faced shell-pink flowers in trusses of about eight opening before the leaves emerge are typical of this plant. A very fine white flowered clone named 'White Find' is worth seeking out. Pinkshell Azaleas flower from April into May, and given enough light can be very floriferous. Of the species I have tried this is the most troublesome and I suspect it may be suffering from a combination of low air humidity and warm soils in the summer months. In 2005, I moved my plant to a cooler, north facing aspect with plenty of sunlight reflected from the sky, and it has shown signs of improvement.

It is in the subseries Luteum that we find the bulk of the American azaleas. Flower colours range from white, through pink and yellow to orange and red.

R. periclymenoides (see next page) is one of several closely allied species. Its large range extends well north of southeast USA, occupying woodlands and stream-sides. Known as 'Pinxterbloom', it forms a twiggy stoloniferous bush, reaching up to 3m when under the canopy of trees. The flowers have long corolla tubes, usually of pink shade, which flare open into white or pink petals with exserted stamens more than twice the length of the tubes. 'Purple' is a rare lavender-purple colour variant. Flowering commences from late April into May as the foliage begins to break and, as alluded to earlier, the flowers are reminiscent of honeysuckle. I first saw this plant blooming in the wild in 2006 in company with *Trillium catesbyi*. As so often with these azaleas, it was a lone plant clinging

KEVIN HUGHES

Rhododendron periclymenoides

to life at the sunny edge of a deciduous woodland fragment. It was the sweet fragrance of its blooms that first drew my attention to it and, as I took photos, I was buzzed by a Ruby-throated Hummingbird that had ownership issues concerning those nectar rich flowers. England is deprived of hummingbirds but both Bee and Hummingbird Hawkmoths find this and its allied species irresistible while they are in flower. In gardens, this is a tough plant and once established can take a dry summer in its stride.

Very similar, differing primarily in its densely glandular corolla tube, is *R. canescens* which is sadly even scarcer in British gardens. Its range covers much of southeast USA, growing primarily in moist woodlands and along streams. The fragrant flowers are very variable, through shades of pink to cream and white. Good forms have been selected in gardens and from the wild, such as the light pink 'Camilla's Blush', 'Varnadoe's Pink' with red tubed pink flowers and 'Varnadoe's Snow', pure white. In the UK it copes well in dry years once it is established, and flowers most prolifically when planted in full sun, though under dappled shade the flower displays are perfectly respectable.

R. prinophyllum is the third member of this set. Its range is more northern, from Quebec south to the Appalachian Mountains, but not down onto the coastal plain. The flowers tend to have shorter corolla tubes and darker pink colours than either *R. periclymenoides* or *R. canescens*. Flowering in the garden is usually May, but up in the mountains such as Dolly Sods Wilderness area in West Virginia the mountaintop will not turn pink until early June.

A much more restricted species is *R. alabamense* (see facing page) from parts of Georgia, Alabama and South Carolina. It mostly favours open deciduous forest and hillsides but I have also found it in flood-plain forest with *Trillium pusillum* var. *alabamense*. This shrub is highly spoken of by all who encounter it. The flowers are white, sometimes with a yellow blotch and not especially large, but strongly fragrant with a hint of spice and lemons. This is not a big species, usually forming a suckering shrub about 1.5m tall. It is closely allied to *R. canescens* and hybrids with that species frequently occur. Again this is a species that benefits from a sunny location in British gardens and will enchant all who are lucky enough to grow it.

The 'Coastal Azalea', *R. atlanticum*, has a large range along the eastern seaboard, from Southern Pennsylvania to Georgia, where

Rhododendron alabamense

it is a characteristic plant of the Pine Barrens. Helped by its suckering habit, it can form extensive colonies, especially on sandy soils. It is usually a small shrub approaching 1m high, typically with white, pink flushed fragrant flowers. Planting in a rock garden or near a pond are good ways to display it and it is a very forgiving plant. Many selections have been named including 'Seaboard', given an Award of Merit when exhibited by the Crown Estate Commissioners on May 25 1964. A group of natural hybrids between *R. atlanticum* and *R. austrinum,* near the Choptank River in Maryland, has given rise to many named forms. Some of the better ones include 'Choptank River' which has deeper pink flowers, 'Marydel' very fragrant white flowers with a hint of pink opening from deep pink and 'Twiggy' a dwarf with white fragrant flowers.

One of the most widespread species is *R. viscosum* into which *R. serrulatum* and *R. oblongifolium* have been included. The range runs south from Maine to Florida and west into Texas. It inhabits swamps and moist mountain slopes and can vary from a 1m to a 4m shrub in the wild. It is also a strongly fragrant species, casting an exotic scent of spices and cloves about the garden. This is also one of the latest rhododendrons to flower in the garden, anywhere between early June–late July. Its vernacular name of 'Swamp Azalea' suggests it might not be ideal for dry gardens and indeed I have found this to be so, but flowering is still better in a sunny location. In early summer 2000 I plunged a dried up plant of 'Crosswater #2' (selected for late shell-pink flowers) into the shallow edge of a pond where I then forgot it. When next I noticed the azalea, winter had arrived and I discovered it had rooted into the gravel of the pond bed. The shrub remained there and flowered prolifically each year. Not an expected pond marginal! Swamp azaleas usually show good autumn colour and, as with the flowers in British gardens, this is enhanced by locating them in a sunny spot. *R. arborescens* is closely related to *R. viscosum* and also has a similar wide distribution but it tends to occupy the mountains to elevations of at least 1500m. It is a larger plant and can make a 5m tree but is more typically seen as a 3m shrub, especially in gardens. It is known as the 'Sweet Azalea' because of its strong cinnamon like fragrance. Blooming from June–July, it is another late flowering species. The flowers are white or pink and usually have noticeable exserted

KEVIN HUGHES

Rhododendron austrinum

Hot colours are signalled by our final set of azaleas from the southeast USA.

R. austrinum, the 'Florida Azalea' (see left) hails from the coastal plains of Georgia, Alabama, Florida and Mississippi where it grows in damp woods and along streams and rivers. One way to see it to perfection is to take a canoe along the rivers, where large 4m specimens grow between the Swamp Cypresses, but be careful as you paddle in for a close look because Water Moccasin snakes like to lie in its overhanging branches. The first time I saw this in the wild was in a fragment of ancient forest in northern Mississippi where it grew with notable plants such as *Magnolia virginiana*, *M. grandiflora*, *M. macrophylla* and *Trillium foetidissimum*. It has fragrant flowers in shades of red through orange to yellow and is thought to be closely allied to *R. canescens*. It is one of the earlier species, the flowers opening before the leaves in late April and May. Good selections include 'Alba' found in northwest Florida, 'Escatawpa' with brilliant orange flowers and 'Pretty One' a large flowered salmon red. It is not a difficult shrub to grow and really likes that sunny spot in the garden. Once established it should not need extra irrigation, even in dry weather.

Even more showy is *R. calendulaceum*, the 'Flame Azalea' (see facing page). It is a native of mountainous country from Pennsylvania to Georgia. The flowers are held

stamens. Good selections have been made and many in the USA declare *R. arborescens* as their favourite species. Clarence Towe named one 'White Lightning', which is spoken of with high regard by Mike Dirr. It has huge white flowers with a yellow blotch, distinctive red stamens and a strong sweet fragrance. Another white flowered form named 'Ailsa' won an Award of Merit in 1952 whilst 'Hot Ginger' leads you to expect the powerful fragrance it delivers in mid-summer.

In contrast to the abundance of *R. arborescens,* the newly described *R. eastmanii* is a very local azalea. Known only from a couple of South Carolina stations, it has a current population of only 500 or so plants. It is a summer flowering fragrant species and surprisingly seems closely allied with *R. occidentale* from the west coast. The flowers are mostly white or cream, usually with a pale yellow blotch and some selected forms have already been made. One of the best of these is 'Charles Eastman' with its pink tipped white bowls and petals.

Rhododendron calendulaceum

KEVIN HUGHES

in loose trusses of five to ten during May and early June. Each flower in the truss can be over 5cm in diameter. They are not fragrant but come in burning colours. I recall the first wild plant I saw on the edge of a small deciduous copse grabbing me by the eyes as I drove past. Each flower contained shades of burnt orange, apricot and salmon red. Mike Dirr describes it as 'abundant in the Southern Appalachians in every imaginable colour' whilst William Bartram summed it up in 1799: 'This is certainly the most gay and brilliant flowering shrub yet known'. There are many good selections, 'Golden Sunset Flame' is one I like, with a blend of orange, gold and yellow colours smouldering in its flowers. In the USA it can be stressed by too much heat but this problem does not seem to trouble us in the UK and again I recommend it for a sunny spot but don't let it get too dry.

A close cousin is *R. flammeum*, the 'Oconee Azalea' which comes from the Piedmont region of Georgia and South Carolina. This species shows a similar range of flower colour but has much narrower, longer corolla tubes giving it an appearance not dissimilar to *R. austrinum* but it is non-scented and flowers later in the season. Unlike the 'Flame Azalea' it is regarded as very heat tolerant. Unfortunately it is the one plant I tried that never established, but I suspect it will prefer a sunny spot in a British woodland garden.

R. bakeri is also closely allied to *R. calendulaceum* and can sometimes be very difficult to separate from it. Its range is relatively isolated to the Cumberland Plateau in Kentucky south to Tennessee and mountains of Georgia, Alabama and North Carolina. Some regard the population on the Cumberland Plateau as a separate species, *R. cumberlandense*. Generally this forms a medium shrub to about 1.8m tall. The flowers in May and June are non-fragrant and mostly in shades of orange. It is a spectacular bush when in its full glory. A very good orange-red form is 'Camp's Red'. In the USA this is not a species regarded as very heat tolerant but in our British climate I have not found this to be a problem. Planted in the shade it gets a bit leggy and is more floriferous in a sunny site.

R. prunifolium, known as the 'Plumleaf Azalea', comes from a localised range in southwest Georgia and east Alabama. Here it grows in shady ravines, often by streams, where its late red flowers light up the forest through July and August on shrubs about 3.5m tall. Colours other than the typical reds also occur, and selections of these include the pinkish orange 'Coral Glow' and the orange form 'Apricot Glow'. Its shiny green glabrous leaves are a perfect foil for its hot colours and with a good background of trees, i.e. lots more green, when even the red flowered forms can look subtle.

R. prunifolium dislikes dry soils and can suffer leaf scorch if given too much exposure to the elements. In British gardens it may not be best suited to the shady sites recommended in the USA, so we do need to make more direct sunshine available. Companion planting of other similar sized shrubs will help to reduce the problems of leaf scorch and indicator herbaceous plants will provide early warning if the ground gets too dry.

Most of these southeast American azaleas are relatively easy to grow and stand up well to what we call summer heat in southern and eastern England. Their flowers are always beautiful and often intensely fragrant, attracting amazing insects such as iridescent Rose Chafer Beetles. Some give good autumn colour and a few are a challenge. Add these to your collection and summer can never be boring in the garden.

References

HH DAVIDIAN. *The Rhododendron Species.* Timber Press

MICHAEL A. DIRR. *Manual of Woody Landscape Plants.* Stipes

FRED C GALLE. *Azaleas.* Timber Press.

Kevin Hughes broadcasts and lectures on a range of horticultural topics and runs Kevin Hughes Plants, based near Lymington in the New Forest, specialising in plants for dry and coastal gardens, and also in his own special interest of woodland plants including trilliums

Rhododendron lacteum and its Hybrids – A Suitable Case For A Reference Collection?

Iris Wright

Among the purists – that is those whose interest in the genus rhododendron is firmly locked into plants defined as species – *Rhododendron lacteum* can send the senses reeling. But while it can obsess, it can also exasperate. By some eminent authorities it has, on the one hand, been described as 'the finest rhododendron ever introduced', 'that diva of the rhododendron world', 'a most wonderful thing' and 'the Monarch of Cangshan'. (Cangshan in WC Yunnan, being where it was first discovered by Delavay and from where it was introduced by George Forrest in 1910). On the other hand it has been deemed slow in growth, reluctant to seed, temperamental and demanding (it is most happy in soil high in acidity, low in nutrients and a cool garden). Perhaps the comment from a very experienced head gardener who had worked with rhododendrons all his life, surpasses them all – '*R. lacteum?* Doesn't flower until it's 40, dies at 50.'

So what we have in *R. lacteum* is a rhododendron which is both highly prized and dismissed in equal measure. Moreover, we have been warned by past commentators that in Britain it is in decline. Yet I know of at least ten gardens (both public and private) in Sussex and Surrey, in southeast England, where *R. lacteum* is growing, so this may not be the case today. If we look at this more closely we find that almost 60 years ago, in the Rhododendron Yearbook 1949, Francis Hanger wrote that '*R. lacteum*... is fast dying out in cultivation'. Thirty years later this view was echoed by Kenneth Lowes, in his well researched article (*Rhododendrons with Magnolias and Camellias 1979–80* p. 64).

Before these articles, there had been only four recorded expeditions by British plant hunters during which *R. lacteum* seed was collected and distributed. Since then, however, there have been at least ten expeditions with British involvement, during which *R. lacteum* seed was collected and returned to the UK.

The question is, how much seed was distributed to British growers prior to 1980 and how much post 1980? What we know is that plants from both pre- and post-1980 collections exist in British gardens today, so this means that the reported decline may not be as alarming as we might have been given to

KENNETH HULME

Rhododendron lacteum at Corsock House, Galloway, Scotland

understand. I am not suggesting there is any room for complacency. Indeed, it would be a most useful exercise to know precisely where in the UK plants of *R. lacteum* are growing, which forms and of what provenance they are, and to record and monitor them. Such knowledge may not only help in maintaining *R. lacteum* as a cultivated plant but perhaps, more importantly, enable pollen to be collected: it should be noted that Kenneth Lowes suggested cross pollinating the best forms of *R. lacteum* in an attempt to increase garden hardiness and flowering on younger plants. According to Kenneth Cox though, this already occurs naturally in the wild.

Rhododendron lacteum has a tight truss of 15–30 flowers which sits very elegantly on an attractive rosette of leaves. It ranges from deep to pale sulphur yellow and to creamy white, either clear or with a red blotch. Its colour does not fade and the flowers last a good two to three weeks, so that over a month or more the plant is covered in beautiful yellow trusses, so unlike many rhododendrons which fade from the second or third day. Last spring (April 2006) my own *R. lacteum* flowered for the first time after a 27-year wait. Was it worth it? Absolutely. It is the Tower Court form and displayed an abundance of finely formed trusses of clear yellow flowers with no red blotch, but beautiful just the same. I counted 34 trusses open or in bud, and through a particularly misty, grey April morning it drew me to itself like a beacon. Previously the plant had started flowering after 20 years but always in October, with tiny, sparse flowers and never a full truss.

The famous and award-winning plants of *R. lacteum* seen in flower in the UK from the 1920s on are, it seems, being propagated but not enough by a long way. The deep yellow, heavily blotched form grown at Corsock is being propagated by David Millais along with those from seed collected by his father, Ted Millais, in 1995 in northeast Yunnan on the Wumengshan, but not yet flowering. The chartreuse yellow, unblotched form of Blackhills, Morayshire, Scotland, purchased as a grafted plant from White's nurseries in 1928 but without a collector's number, died about 15 years ago, but two layers from it have meant that this lovely plant lives on there – the layers now good sized flowering plants. Several other forms of *R. lacteum* grow at Blackhills including two that were purchased from Peter Cox at Glendoick

Rhododendron 'Lionel's Triumph' at Exbury

PHILIP DE ROTHSCHILD

Nurseries, which flowered after 8 years. These are from seed collected through the 1981 Sino-British Expedition to Cangshan, numbered SBEC0235 and SBEC0345, and were supplied as grafted plants. John Christie of Blackhills is delighted to report that they "have proved particularly good – free flowering and almost blotch free". Stephen Fox, gardening in Derbyshire, also acquired SBEC0345 during the autumn of 1986. It flowered in the spring of 2002 and has continued since.

The 'Blackhills' FCC 1965 form (Frontispiece colour photo *The Rhododendron and Camellia Yearbook 1968*) is similar to the Royal Botanic Garden Edinburgh form, from Forrest 6778 – a clear, waxy, thick textured, yellow that shines out from a distance. Unfortunately the RBGE plant is now dead. The plant at Logan (part of RBGE) still flowers reliably, as does that at Wakehurst in Sussex. These won many prizes for their respective owners, Olaf Hambro and Sir Henry Price. Three specimens of *R. lacteum* can be found in the Valley Gardens at Windsor but the original and best *R. lacteum* at Exbury has died, although others there are still flowering. I visited the garden at Werrington Park last year but cannot recall seeing their F6778 FCC 1926 form flowering.

There are those who may want to grow *R. lacteum* but simply do not want to wait up to 30 years for it to flower. One answer is to grow *R. lacteum* as a grafted plant which does hasten flowering. The Cox family at Glendoick Nurseries graft onto *R. calophytum* or *R. calophytum* hybrid stock, and all I have spoken to growing *R. lacteum* purchased from them have experienced flowering on younger plants.

As long as gardeners are not 'species only' collectors, consolation can also lie in the *R. lacteum* hybrids. Although *R. lacteum* may be difficult to grow from seed or too long to wait for, as a parent it has proved to be excellent. The mystery, though, is why *R. lacteum* has not been used far more extensively to produce what could be a sensational range of plants.

I grow two Tower Court hybrids near their Tower Court parent. The first is *R.* 'John Barr Stevenson' (*R. lacteum* × 'Logan Damaris' AM 1948) and this flowers before the species. It retains the same luminous yellow truss and is a fine and reliable plant, flowering at seven years and ever since. The second is *R.* 'Robert Keir'

IRIS WRIGHT

Rhododendron 'Robert Keir' growing at Kilsaran, Crowborough 2006

(*R. lacteum* × 'Luscombei') (see above) named after Roza Stevenson's head gardener at Tower Court. The flowers are pale cream and yellow-suffused rose, sit up on a beautiful rosette of leaves, inherited from the parent, and took 14 years to flower. Another Tower Court hybrid is *R.* 'Beatrice Keir' AGM. This, named after Robert Keir's wife, is of the same cross as 'John Barr Stevenson', has thick and waxy flowers and is the most readily available in the trade. Another, from the other cross, is the oddly named *R.* 'Lactcombei' – no prizes for guessing its parents, but where would you find it today?

We have both Lionel and Edmund de Rothschild of Exbury to thank for many excellent hybrids of *R. lacteum*. One of the best is *R.* 'Repose' AM 1956 (*R. discolor* × *R. lacteum*) creamy yellow with a tiny green throat, looking very like its parent. *R.* 'Mariloo' (*R.* 'Dr Stocker' × *R. lacteum*) is a compact, pure yellow truss like its parent and, I believe, long lived, although my own plant flowered at six years and died at twelve. Preferable is *R.* 'Mariloo Eugenie' AM 1950 and *R.* 'Mariloo Gilbury' AM 1943. *R.* 'Joanita' was a result of crossing *R. lacteum* with *R. campylocarpum* subsp. *caloxanthum* and reversed as *R.* 'Costa del Sol' AM 1969. (I have not seen 'Costa del Sol', but one grower of it mentioned it was a poor doer for him.) *R.* 'Endeavour' (*R. arboreum* var. *album* × *R. lacteum*) and *R.* 'Jason' AM 1966 (*R. lacteum* × *R.* 'Penjerrick') (see facing page) are very garden-worthy plants. Lionel de Rothschild used *R. calophytum* with *R. lacteum* to great effect in *R.* 'Galactic' AM 1964, FCC 1970 (*R.* 'Avalanche' [*R. calophytum* × 'Loderi'] × *R. lacteum*) and *R.* 'Jocelyne' AM 1954, FCC 1956 (*R. lacteum* × *R. calophytum*). Then there is the very beautiful and sumptuous *R.* 'Lionel's Triumph' AM (*R. lacteum R.* 'Naomi') (see previous page). This hybrid is half *R. lacteum*, a quarter *R. fortunei* plus *R. griffithianum* and *R. thomsonii*, and is the deepest yellow of all the hybrids of *R. lacteum*. The plant can be straggly but the compensation is the superb flower truss. Edmund de Rothschild then crossed *R.* 'Lionel's Triumph' back with *R.* 'Naomi Exbury' and produced another winner in *R.* 'Elizabeth de Rothschild' AM 1965. In recent years, Exbury placed several *R.* 'Lionel's First' (*R. lacteum* × *R. sutchuenense*) on the showbench at the Early Rhododendron Show in London and won first prize in all the classes entered. Glendoick Nurseries are selling *R. lacteum* × *R. taliense*, a naturally occurring hybrid on the Cangshan.

There have been other sources of hybrids – *R.* 'Hilde' (*R. fulvum* × *R. lacteum*) by JB Stevenson; *R.* 'Lacs' (*R. lacteum* × *R. sinogrande)* by Magor 1936; *R.* 'Middlemarch' AM from Borde Hill – but where are they now? Many of the hybrids named above are difficult, if not impossible, to obtain. It is quite extraordinary that, after waiting to see a hybrid of *R. lacteum* flower, registered and award-winning plants are allowed to disappear. Would the Americans allow this to happen? The Rhododendron Species Foundation in Seattle list several forms of *R. lacteum* and its hybrids from British and other sources, which they make commercially available.

On the other hand, how far is too far when hybridising *R. lacteum*? I noted this hybrid on the web (*R. maximum* × *R.* 'Sir Charles Lemon') × (*R.* 'Fawn' × *R.* 'Repose').

The Rhododendron, Camellia and Magnolia Group have put together plant collections of large-leaved rhododendrons, hardy hybrids, Kunming camellias and × *loebneri* magnolias. Would members of the Group favour a 'safe' collection of the best forms of *R. lacteum* and its hybrids? Currently there are plants growing from seed collected post-1980 by Keith Rushforth, Roy Lancaster, Alan Clarke, Ted Millais, Peter Cox, Peter Hutchison, Patrick Forde, Maurice Foster (two in my own garden) and others, besides those pre-1940 of Forrest, Kingdon Ward, McLaren and Rock. Also, there are those

PHILIP DE ROTHSCHILD

Rhododendron 'Jason' at Exbury

collected and growing in the North America and Europe. The best of these, growing together, would provide an exquisite scene, and pollen and grafting material would be available for future generations. Or is that too ambitious? I hope not.

On the other hand, aficionados would probably quote Lionel de Rothschild "No other rhododendron has a more perfect truss" (Rhododendron Yearbook 1953, p.55) or Kenneth Cox "If you want the best yellow rhododendron you want *R. lacteum* itself."

Iris Wright is a member of the Southeast Branch of the Group and, with her husband Brian, has developed a specialist collection of rhododendrons, camellias and magnolias at their garden in Crowborough, Sussex, which has produced many winners at RHS competitions

Taxonomy Topics

Maurice Foster

Camellia confusion clarified

Although *Camellia yunnanensis* (section Protocamellia Chang 1996) and *C. henryana* (section Pseudocamellia Sealy 1958) are classified in different sections of the genus, the two species are often confused.

Although *C. henryana* flowers in early spring and *C. yunnanensis* usually in autumn, some forms of the latter have an unusually long season and continue into early spring; and other individuals flower in the spring instead of the autumn and can be taken for *C. henryana*. The two species share very similar botanical characteristics.

Both taxa can make large shrubs or trees to about 7m with villous young shoots; both have similar foliage, with leaves serrate, acuminate and cuneate or rounded at the base, with short pubescent petioles. Both have white flowers, borne at the tip of the shoot and in the upper axils. Those of *C. yunnanensis* are occasionally but not always larger, from 3–9cm across, compared to *C. henryana* from 3–5cm.

The number of petals varies only marginally, with 8–12in *C. yunnanensis* and 7–10in *C. henryana*. Generally obovate, they are united from the base to the staminal column. Both the androecium, the male flower component, and the gynoecium, the female element, are essentially the same in both species, except for the number of styles. This

MAURICE FOSTER

Camellia henryana

MAURICE FOSTER

Camellia yunnanensis

marks an important character in identification with *C. yunnanensis* having four–seven styles while *C. henryana* has only three.

The other significant difference is with the capsules. Both are globose, but those of *C. yunnanensis* can be very large, to 8cm in diameter and up to twice the size of *C. henryana*. Those of the former are purple-red and very decorative at maturity; those of the latter a smooth green. However, the substantive difference is in the thickness of the pericarp. In *C. yunnanensis* the capsule wall is extremely thick, up to 2cm, compared to the meagre 0.2cm in *C. henryana.*

Thus in flower and in fruit the two species can quite readily be separated, but identification remains difficult in the absence of both. The bark of both is smooth, but in mature *C. yunnanensis* is often a very beautiful rusty brown.

The picture is further complicated by a close ally of *C. henryana*, a third very similar species, *C. trichocarpa*. Ming (2000) reduces this to a variety of *C. henryana*, with pubescent instead of glabrous ovaries. Group members who have seen this flowering in warm temperate conditions in Australia and New Zealand extol the decorative virtues of a small tree to 4m with abundant white flowers beautifully and plentifully displayed. Dr Clifford Parks recommends extensive planting of this attractive plant in areas where the temperature does not fall below –6°C.

I have found both *C. yunnanensis* and *C. henryana* to be excellent species for pot, conservatory or cool greenhouse cultivation and forms of *C. yunnanensis*, which ranges occasionally up to 3000m in Yunnan and southwest Sichuan, could be worth trying outside, given our recent run of mild winters. I have not yet been bold enough to do so.

Source

Collected species of the genus camellia – an illustrated outline Cao Jiyin, Clifford R Parks, Du Yueqiang.

Maurice Foster is a former Chairman of the Group, and currently a member of the Executive Committee. He is also a member of the RHS Woody Plants Committee. He has made many plant trips to China and elsewhere

FORGOTTEN PLANTS
RHODODENDRON 'FAIRYLIGHT'

PHILIP EVANS

If one grows mainly rhododendron species, extending the rhododendron flowering season into June can be a challenge. In our Cornish woodland garden there are *Rhododendron elliottii, R. dichroanthum* and *R. discolor,* plus late-flowering forms of both *R. decorum* and *R. crassum* – with *R. auriculatum* to come in July/August. But the best value is splendid *R. griersonianum*, which unfailingly lights us through the whole of June and into early July with its shining geranium-pink trumpets. *Griersonianum* must be about the most hybridised of all species. The last *RHS Rhododendron Hybrids Handbook* (1969) listed 154 *griersonianum* crosses, and I imagine there have been some additions in the intervening 37 years. The one drawback of griersonianum can be its lax habit, and this is perhaps a case where, judged purely as a garden ornamental plant, a number of its hybrids are an improvement on the species. One of the best, is *R.* 'Winsome', but it is really a May flowerer. *R.* 'Fabia' is later, but makes rather a leggy plant. Others that flower well into June are 'Vulcan', 'Romany Chai' and 'Vanessa', and are all good.

Two less familiar hybrids we planted were *R.* 'Daydream' ('Lady Bessborough' × *griersonianum*) and *R.* 'Fairylight', both of Exbury origin. Unfortunately, *R.* 'Daydream' got washed away in 2004, on the day of the 'Boscastle flood' precipitation, but *R.* 'Fairylight' survived and is making a compact, not too dense plant with oblanceolate leaves that are elegant, and well poised.

Prior to the Group AGM at Wisley on 13 June this year (2006),

MIKE ROBINSON

Rhododendron 'Fairylight' on Battleston Hill, RHS Garden Wisley

Colin Crosbie (Superintendent of Woody Plants) took members on a tour of Battleston Hill. By that date it was the cornus display that took pride of place, but outstanding amongst rhododendrons still in flower was a large specimen of *R.* 'Fairylight' at its best. Our Chairman kindly took a photo of it, and this is reproduced here, to support its case.

Rhododendron 'Fairylight' was a Lionel de Rothschild introduction around 1948. It is stated to be *griersonianum* × 'Lady Mar'. 'Lady Mar' was probably an Exbury hybrid, although it is not recorded in the 1979 revised edition of the Lucas Phillips & Barber *The Rothschild Rhododendrons* and the new revised *RHS International Rhododendron Register* describes its parentage as unknown. But I suspect that 'Lady Mar' had *R. fortunei* in its genes.

Cox's Encyclopedia says there are two clones of 'Fairylight', one a darker pink than the other, and considers it similar to 'Vanessa'. However, I feel 'Fairylight' has real individual merit. Both flowers and foliage I find superior to 'Vanessa', and the flowers a better shape and colour than the *griersonianum-fortunei discolor* cross, *R.* 'Azor'.

Rhododendron 'Fairylight' is therefore my nomination for this year's 'Forgotten Plant,' although since the *RHS Plant Finder* shows it as available from two well known specialist nurseries, possibly a more accurate description might be 'should be better known'.

Philip Evans is Honorary Editor of this Yearbook

Book Reviews

Hardy Rhododendron Species: a guide to identification.
James Cullen. Timber Press, 2005 £35.

James Cullen has written many clear, authoritative and widely used texts. The publication in spring 2006 of a book by him, addressed to the lay person, on the identification of rhododendron species, was an exciting event.

His book begins with a nicely summarised general introduction and history, plus sketches (somewhat idealised as usual) of the hairs and scales that can be seen of leaf laminae under a laboratory microscope. The botanists' keys for distinguishing subgenera and sections follow, with the subsections of Hymenanthes dealt with first, followed by azaleas, other elepidote sections and finishing with the lepidote species.

Each subsection begins with a key to the species. In the case of lepidotes these are very similar to the author's 1980 revision and similar keys are written out for the other sections. The treatment of a few subsections is very subjective – only four species of subsection Barbata being mentioned with the old name of *Rhododendron smithii* being used.

Each species is described in about half a page. The descriptions are brief and clear, but lack the anecdotal comments to make the text more approachable and useful. About 10% of the descriptions are accompanied with photographs, of which those showing the detail of parts of the plant are excellent.

Within the usual features of each description there is a bibliography of all published illustrations of each species. Where this is known, the source of plants in cultivation is noted, and a statement is made as to whether the cultivated material is authenticated (but not by whom).

So far, the book adopts the traditional approach of a botanist to the subject. However, the most significant feature is towards the end, where the author has valiantly prepared a number of tables to assist identification by enthusiasts and horticulturalists (as opposed to botanists and those who have made a study of herbarium specimens). The tables inevitably contain the words 'generally' or 'usually' but this is no criticism – identification is not an exact science, especially as natural hybrids may well be involved.

The division into sections is a precise and clear summary. The division into subsections is less clear, and it is unfortunate that the first entry in the first table on Hymenanthes involves flower characteristics. So often an attempt has to be made to identify, or to get near to identifying, a plant that is not in flower: the approach in this book betrays the author's background as a botanist rather than a grower. It also quickly becomes evident that many species are missing from the tables, and that the book has ignored most of the taxonomy done and species introduced since the author's retirement.

This reviewer attempted to use the tables, with some success, but when trying to key out *R. wardii,* he ended up with *R. decorum*; another attempt to reach *R. ciliicalyx* ended up with *R. dendricola*. Of course the attempt to create tables of this kind is an extremely difficult task and the author is to be commended for his efforts, but such failures were rather off-putting, and might well discourage a beginner completely.

The ultimate question about the book is whether it provides a better guide to identification of species than previous publications. On balance this reviewer thinks not: too many species are omitted, the species descriptions lack entertaining and useful anecdotal notes, there are far too few photographs and the tables are by no means infallible.

On the other hand, the easily available references to illustrations of species and the note on the provenance of authenticated species in cultivation are very useful. It might have been useful to print the identification tables in a separate and portable form.

I think that the Coxs' *Encyclopedia of Rhododendron Species* is still by far the best one volume text on this subject.

Mike Robinson

Rhododendrons of subgenus Vireya
Dr George Argent
Royal Horticultural Society in association with the Royal Botanic Garden Edinburgh
ISBN 1-902896-61-0 £55

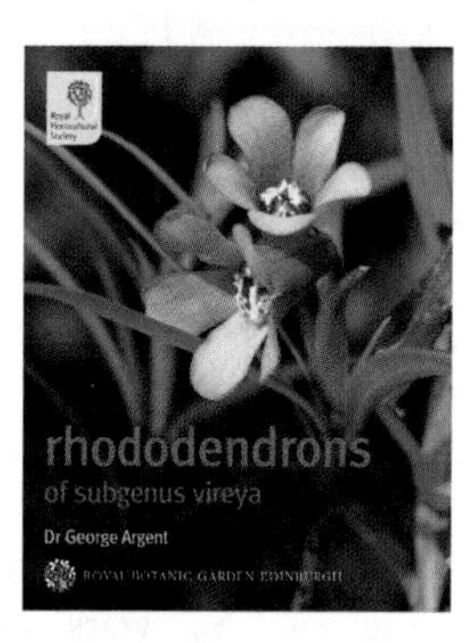

For the past forty years, those with an interest in vireya rhododendron species have had to rely on the classic account by Professor Hermann Sleumer published in 1966 as part of *Flora Malesiana*, and later reprinted as *An Account of Rhododendron in Malesia*, as their principal point of reference. It is unsurprising, therefore, that Dr Argent's revision has been eagerly anticipated since word of its production first emerged several years ago and I am pleased to report that readers of this new book will be generously rewarded for their patience.

Dr Argent, who has recently retired from his role as Senior Tropical Botanist with the Royal Botanic Garden Edinburgh, is acknowledged as the world's foremost authority on vireya rhododendrons. He first became interested in this group of plants in 1977 and since that time has undertaken numerous field trips to South East Asia from where he has introduced many vireya species, currently in cultivation as part of the superb Living Collection at the RBGE.

This extensive first-hand knowledge of the plants, both in the field and in cultivation, has enabled Dr Argent to review and greatly expand upon the botanical descriptions of the species given in *Flora Malesiana*, based on living, rather than herbarium material as was largely the case in Sleumer's account. It is these descriptions that comprise the bulk, and principal purpose of this new volume – a total of 313 species set out over 300 pages, including a number of new taxa published here for the first time. A 'Key to the Sections and Subsections within Subgenus *Vireya*' precedes the descriptive accounts and further 'Keys to the Species' are also provided at the head of each Section. Accompanying the detailed descriptive data for each taxon are notes containing useful supplementary information. These variously cover, the plant's status in cultivation, its introduction, related species together with distinctive characteristics to look out for in such cases, naturally occurring hybrids and an explanation of any changes in taxonomic rank since Sleumer.

Photographs of around 150 species, a small number of which appear to have unfortunately suffered at the hands of the printers, are included in this chapter of the book, a mix of both the more widely available and the lesser known, amply illustrating the wide variation in flower form and colour seen within this group of plants.

Prior to commenting on the remaining chapters of the book, mention must be made at this point of Dr Argent's, possibly somewhat controversial, decision to raise *Vireya* to the status of subgenus within *Rhododendron* as set out in the introduction to his revision. As the author points out in the conspectus of classification, this is not a new idea and has been proposed on several occasions over the years, most recently by Professor Spethmann (1980, 1987). Dr Argent gives two principal reasons for following this course: firstly it 'recognises the distinctness of the group' – it is a clearly defined unit within *Rhododendron* with 'no intermediates or species that are doubtfully placed'. Secondly, bearing in mind that Dr Argent's work closely follows Sleumer's classification – which itself is artificial in concept (based on morphology rather than phylogeny, i.e. leaf and flower characteristics rather than evolutionary relationships) – raising the status to subgenus is essentially practical, allowing for more appropriate use of subdivisions below this rank. Further arguments are presented, citing recent research, giving good morphological grounds for separating the vireyas including the unique presence of large idioblasts in the leaves (Nilsen, 2003) and distinct ovary, ovule and mega-gametophyte characters (Palser *et al*, 1991), as well as the long-established tailed seed characteristic.

As a result of raising *Vireya* to the rank of subgenus, all former subsections have been promoted to the level of section with the exception of *Solenovireya*, which has effectively been demoted as it remains a subsection, now moved to within the large section *Euvireya*. The principal defining characteristic of *Solenovireya*, flower shape (trumpet-shaped, white or pale pink, the lobes less than a quarter of the length of the tube, as seen in the popular *Rhododendron jasminiflorum*), is considered too weak to be maintained at sectional level.

One further change to the classification by Dr Argent, is the introduction of *Discovireya* at sectional level, a name first proposed by Prof. Sleumer in his 1949 classification. This did not feature in *Flora Malesiana*, which dealt only with species occurring within the botanical region of Malesia, thereby omitting the outlying vireyas found on mainland Asia. Essentially, Dr Argent has split the former subsection *Pseudovireya*, which, whilst retained and raised, now includes only those species found on the mainland (India, Taiwan, Vietnam and China), with the majority, those from the islands of the Malesian region, being moved into *Discovireya*.

Following on from the Introduction, Dr Argent devotes a short chapter to 'A History of *Vireya*', from the first published description of a vireya, *Rhododendron malayanum*, by William Jack in 1822, through the early collections of explorers like Thomas Lobb and Charles Curtis, the ground-breaking work of George Henslow and Herbert Copeland, to Prof. Hermann Sleumer's revision for *Flora Malesiana*. Whilst much of this is documented elsewhere, Dr Argent has taken the opportunity to record developments over the last 50 years by acknowledging the contributions made by members of the scientific community, enthusiastic amateur growers and dedicated small-scale, specialist nurserymen.

The remaining three chapters of the book deal with 'Collecting and Conservation', 'Cultivation and Propagation' and 'Pests, Diseases and Disorders'. In the first, Dr Argent gives us a brief glimpse into the world of the modern day plant hunter, with its emphasis on responsible collecting and protection of natural habitats.

The second chapter is written by David Mitchell and Louise Galloway of the Royal Botanic Garden Edinburgh and is the product of their vast experience in maintaining the vireya collection at the Garden. Much useful advice is to be gleaned here by the amateur grower, although some of the cultivation requirements suggested may need to be adapted (e.g. shading), or even disregarded (e.g. supplementary lighting), to take account of local growing conditions by readers in more favourable climates than northern Europe. The final chapter has again been written by a member of the RBGE staff, Stephan Helfer, and covers a multitude of potential pitfalls that could befall one's vireyas, accompanied by some useful photographs of afflicted plants for reference.

The book closes with a seven-page glossary of botanical terms used therein; followed by six pages of line drawings to illustrate the various leaf shapes, scale types, etc. seen in *Vireya*. The 'References' appendix, with its extensive list of literature cited throughout the book, leaves the enthusiastic reader with much to investigate.

By including a good selection of photographs, together with chapters on the history of *Vireya*, collecting and conservation, cultivation and propagation, and pests and diseases, Dr Argent and his publishers, the RHS, have moved away from the customarily rather 'dry' monograph of years gone by, towards a more user-friendly, all-encompassing volume that should appeal to a wider audience. It could perhaps be argued, however, that with a cover price of £55, the book is unlikely to appeal to the newcomer to vireyas looking for cultural information, most of which is covered in other publications, and these pages might have been better-used. Expanding the notes accompanying the individual species descriptions to include further information on each taxon would have been one option, (many of Dr Argent's own papers describing new species, in journals such as *The New Plantsman*, run to several pages each), with more species represented by a photograph, preferably in a slightly larger format. A set of distribution maps with lists of species found in each of the island groups of the region would also have been welcome.

Dr Argent, in his introductory comments, acknowledges the molecular work carried out by various parties over recent years, but appears cautious in accepting some of the findings at this stage, and states that 'the present work is not trying to represent evolution or monophyly but to present a practical way of dividing this large group of species into subunits so that species can be identified'. This he has surely achieved and in the process given us an indispensable guide to the vireyas. The timely publication of the book seems appropriate, bringing the morphology-based classification of *Vireya* right up to date just as advances in molecular research gather pace. As further DNA analysis is undertaken, and a wider range of taxa sampled, an alternative classification based on the phylogeny of *Vireya* will undoubtedly emerge, at which time a better comparison will be possible between the author's morphological classification and the evolutionary relationships of *Vireya* uncovered from such research – fascinating times ahead!

So, how would this reviewer sum up the book? To borrow a much over-used phrase, which in this case I believe genuinely appropriate, it is 'essential reading' for anyone with an interest in vireyas; or, indeed, rhododendrons in general, bearing in mind that the vireyas represent around one-third of the genus. It is the first full account of *Vireya* to be published and, judging by the fact that the initial print run was almost fully allocated through advance orders alone, is already considered the new standard reference work. The book will do much to stimulate interest in these plants, as the lack of easy access to relevant authoritative literature has for many years undoubtedly been a barrier to a greater awareness of the group.

Chris Callard
www.vireya.net

Group Tour to Canada and the USA

Overview – Rosemary Legrand

A group of 24 members made an unforgettable tour to some of the most outstanding private and public gardens of Vancouver, Victoria, Port Ludlow, Seattle/Tacoma, Portland/Eugene and finally San Francisco. Charlie Sale from Vancouver masterminded our excellent itinerary. It included many of the private gardens of his personal friends and he provided us with enlightening and fascinating information about each garden that he described with his own inimitable enthusiasm.

Glen Patterson's Roof Garden, Vancouver (18 April 2006)

On the evening of our arrival, our first garden set the standard for our tour; Glen Patterson, our charming host, generously welcomed us to his superb Japanese-style roof garden with panoramic views over the water and mountains beyond.

It took Glen over three years to prepare the plants that he had selected to move from his former large garden. A striking red 100-year-old Japanese Maple created a glorious focal point. Dwarf rhododendrons, and an established *Rhododendron macabeanum* 'Earl of Stair' form, and *R.* 'Lady Alice Fitzwilliam' were in flower. I even noticed an *Acacia pravissima* growing amongst a fine collection of shrubs and alpines.

155 High View Place, Lions Bay BC
250 Oceanview Road, Lions Bay BC
Charlton/Sale Garden, North Vancouver (19 April 2006)

Grey weather conditions did not dampen our enthusiasm as we encountered the steep, narrow woodland paths in the 1-acre garden of Richard Mossakowski, with views of distant snow-covered mountain peaks. The garden's sparse soil is covered with moss with yellow native violas and a superb prostrate *R. forrestii* var. *repens* growing beneath a varied collection of rhododendrons, including *R. fulvum*, *R. scabrifolium*, *R.* 'Sir Charles Lemon' and, most noteworthy, a lovely dwarf *R. dendrocharis* from Sichuan with rose pink blooms.

Within a short walking distance was the rugged two and a third acre woodland garden of Joseph and Joanne Ronsley. Joe was President of the Rhododendron Species Foundation Board of Directors and, despite recovering from recent surgery, he gamely escorted us around his exciting garden, which was home to a fine collection of rhododendron species amongst them *R. falconeri* and *R. oreodoxa* var. *fargesii* with funnel shaped watercolour-pink flowers. In this garden we first encountered *R.* 'Malahat', a glowing scarlet hybrid and the native *Arbutus menziesii* with its cinnamon-coloured peeling bark. The steep valley and waterfall provided an excellent habitat for rhododendrons and camellias.

The warm hospitality and delightful refreshments offered to us by these two garden owners was repeated when we were privileged to enjoy a delicious lunch in the home of Charlie and Margaret Sale, before we explored their treasure trove garden of rare and diverse plants. We saw epimediums, particularly *Epimedium leptorrhizum* from the 60 varieties in Margaret's collection, the opulent *Cypripedium formosanum*, exquisite little *Kalmiopsis fragrans*, species rhododendrons and the eye-catching waxy red blooms of hybrid *R.* 'Maxine Childers', to name but a few. All excel in the rocky woodland conditions where a *Magnolia campbellii* was encouraged to bloom by Roy Lancaster and Margaret's nimble footwork.

During the evening, Peter Wharton delivered an awe-inspiring lecture with slides of a recent plant hunting expedition to North Vietnam and the Phan Si Pan massif, which has 15,000 hectares of national parks. This is undoubtedly one of today's most intriguing countries, offering thrilling new plant discoveries.

UBC Botanical Garden; Van Dusen Botanical Garden (20 April 2006)

After three mountain-goat steep woodland gardens, it was very pleasant to visit a level sea-side garden on a bluff 200 ft high. It is a huge 44 hectares (110 acres). There are no strong winds here; the garden is protected by the bluff, and the north wind blows over the top.

We only saw the 12-hectare David C Lam Asiatic Garden, and were very pleased to be led by Peter Wharton, Curator, who had given us a talk the previous evening on plant hunting in Northern Vietnam. The UBC policy is to propagate species for conservation; to be a museum of anthropology; and to build stocks so that they can be re-planted in the wild in their countries of origin.

With the exception of three clones of *Magnolia cylindrica* (the true species) and a wonderful New Zealand mollicomata hybrid 'Bernie Hollard', the magnolias were over: there is a large collection mainly of species.

The rhododendron collection is integrated with native plants and ground cover – ferns, native and exotic. The older hybrids are being replaced with recent wild collected material. Peter Wharton knows the derivation of each plant, where and when collected and by whom. Among the plants pointed out were *R. augustinii* 'Peter Kerr', a group of *R. coeloneuron* Sich 1198 in flower, *R. concinnum, R. hodgsonii* aff CHM 3093, *R. luteiflorum*, *R. ochraceum* in flower, *R. patulum*, an early Farrer collection of *R. rubiginosum*, *R. sanguineum* var. *cloiophorum*, *R. sinofalconeri* SEH229, *R. thomsonii* BLM 1971 and the unnamed triflora PW20.

Other genera are well represented, with recent collections again to the fore. We passed a styrax sp. with reflexed white and salmon pink petals, *Melliodendron xylocarpum*, maples collected by Mark Flanagan and Tony Kirkham, evergreen magnolias from south China, *Styrax tonkinensis* from Tom Hudson, *Sorbus thibetica* from Keith Rushforth plus the not so recent *Camellia reticulata* from E.H. Wilson.

The most memorable 'other genera' plants were *Carpinus fangiana*, a new large-leaved plum-bronze hornbeam from north Hunan: the photograph on the front cover of Peter Wharton's book *The Jade Garden* shows just how remarkable this is, and, perhaps best of all, *Staphylea holocarpa* var. *rosea* EN 3625.

The collection is a masterpiece of outstanding new plants and a veritable *Who's Who* of plant collectors.

Joey Warren

Van Dusen Botanical Garden, Vancouver Dr M Bale's Garden, Harrison Lookout, Vancouver (20 April 2006)

A most popular botanical garden with seven lakes surrounded by a vast collection of shrubs and trees. The magnolias were in full bloom, with many fine species and hybrids planted together. Ghostly white *Betula utilis* var. *jacquemontii* were grouped with purple *R. concinnum*. Vivid *R. augustinii* 'Marion Mac' created a blue haze, and the black-crimson blooms of *R. sanguineum* subsp. *didymum* contrasted with the pale flaking bark of *Betula albosinensis*. The star attraction on the day of our visit was most probably a very handsome *R.* 'Grace Seabrook' in full flower.

We continued our journey to the extensive garden of Dr Michael Bale, a local GP, who is creating the ultimate rhododendron garden with thousands of rhododenrons planted in 25 acres on a mountain ridge site, situated in an excellent growing region where one magnolia grower ships 10,000, 5ft to 7 ft plants per year.

Dr Bale himself has a very productive propagation unit and nursery which, together with some dramatic new plantings, made this garden a must to re-visit in the future. We were entertained to a most welcome barbecue which gave us the opportunity to talk to Dr Bale and his team.

It would be neglectful of me not to mention the choice trees selected in Vancouver and Vancouver Island for municipal plantings. *Acer palmatum* and cornus are widely used, spring bulbs and flowering plants provide a kaleidoscope of colour in the formal beds. The local population respect and cherish their gardens: no vandalism was apparent.

Darts Hill; Carmen Varcoe's Garden, Victoria (21 April 2006)

Darts Hill is described in a separate article by Graham Laine (see page 46).

After a stunning scenic ferry crossing to Vancouver Island we arrived at Carmen Varcoe's garden.

Dappled sunlight gave this garden a pleasing cool atmosphere, the perfect setting for the comprehensive selection of bulbs and perennials, which complemented the rhododendrons, camellias and magnolias. Star-like *Anemone nemorosa* 'Vestal' and *Narcissus* 'Papillon' were in flower, but the plant that intrigued us most was *Clematis recta* 'Serious Black' with purple-black foliage. *R. bureavii* × *yakushimanum* with sumptuous foliage and bright red shoots was of particular note, as was *R. heliolepis* with its pretty trusses of lavender rose blooms. *Darmera peltata*, the Indian rhubarb, was flourishing close to the pond in this delightful plantswoman's garden.

The Abkhazi Garden; private gardens of Valerie Murray and Hella Vaartnou; University of Victoria, Finnerty Gardens (22 April 2006)

The Abkhazi is a gem. Beautifully maintained by Valerie Murray, the curator, and a keen team of volunteers, it was the creation of Princess Peggy Abkhazi in the mid-1940s. The natural stone outcrops and mature oaks contribute to the flowing landscape design within this $1^1/_2$-acre site. Brilliant jewel colours from the

ROSEMARY LEGRAND

Abkhazi Garden

deciduous and evergreen azaleas, the rich tones of *Acer palmatum* var. *dissectum* 'Garnet', ferns, primulas, a superb double white *Trillium kurabayashii*, *Chamaecyparis nootkatensis* 'Green Arrow' and evergreen ground-covering *Arctostaphylos uva-ursi* will long remain in my memory of the Abkhazi.

It was only a short distance to Lansdowne Road and the private garden of Valerie Murray that contained a collection of unusual plants, many grown in pots and most artistically arranged. Dark bronze *Aeonium foliis purpureis* and podophyllum were displayed with ornamental grasses and agaves.

Adjoining Valerie's property is that of Hella Vaartnou, whose late husband was passionate about rhododendrons and had planted a fine collection in yet another woodland setting with a fabulous plant of *R.* 'Mi Amor', a hybrid between *lindleyi* and *nuttallii* to welcome us in the front garden, and exquisite groups of pleione orchids among the rhododendrons in the rear garden.

During the afternoon we arrived in glorious spring sunshine at the University of Victoria, Finnerty Gardens. The whole area had formerly been logged by the Hudson Bay Company and these gardens have increased from the original 2 acres to the present 6½ acres. In 1973 the rhododendron garden was started by the Buchanan Simpsons who were the owners. It is now a trust run by a management board. The garden is open to the public and melts into the surroundings as it has an open plan design. Some very mature *Arbutus menziesii* stand in the car park. In the gardens we found *Michelia chapensis* from North Vietnam and a huge specimen of *R. yunnanense* in full bloom towering above us, which was an amazing sight. *Betula ermanii*

'Grayswood Hill' had outstanding white bark and amongst the rhododendron collection was a very mature *R.* 'Loderi Venus' which looked fabulous in full flower. Finally to leave these gardens without a mention of the beautiful warm pink blooms of *R.* 'Buchanan Simpson' would be remiss.

Private garden of Elaine and David Whitehead; 'Deep Cove', the private garden of Ruth and John Trelawney; 'Towner Crest', the garden of Evelyn and Nick Weesjes, Victoria (23 April 2006)

Elaine and David Whitehead's immaculate 1-acre garden is 12 years old. It has inspirational garden design features with specimen trees like *Cornus controversa* 'Variegata', a splendid *R. williamsianum*, a great collection of choice perennials, and when we visited, there was a breathtaking display of golden yellow tulips which reflected the bright sunshine of the day. Wide, sloping grass paths meandered past island beds down to the pebble beach with water frontage and unspoilt views of the tree-lined landscape and distant mountains; an idyllic setting for any garden.

'Deep Cove' is a true plantsman's garden, where over the years Ruth and John Trelawney have established a woodland planting brimming with rhododendrons, camellias, magnolias and varied ornamentals. On the south-facing aspect of their garden, illustrating the temperate weather conditions on Vancouver Island, are many Australasian plants which thrive in this region. These include the beautiful and tender *Grevillea rosmarinifolia* and dwarf *Hebe raoulii,* from South Island, New Zealand, which has lilac

ROSEMARY LEGRAND

Elaine and David Whitehead's garden in Victoria

rosette shaped flowers and serrated red edged leaves. Both of these flourish at Deep Cove, which overlooks Finlayson Arm and the Gulf Islands. Sadly, we just did not have enough time in this special garden.

We continued our travels, reaching Towner Crest in the afternoon for a warm welcome from Evelyn Weesjes, who shared with us her extensive and unsurpassed private collection of rhododendron species and hybrids, magnolias and camellias. Originally a 10-acre Hop Farm of which up to seven acres are now planted as a garden.

The rose-pink blooms of *R.* 'Elize Weesjes' looked most attractive. *R.* 'Diane' a pale lemon with a compact truss together with *R. davidsonianum* Exbury form, *R. oreotrephes*, *R. spinuliferum* and *R. sinogrande* (Brodick form) succeed admirably.

I was interested to see *Blechnum pennamarina* making good groundcover, and amongst the hosta collection a small lime green *Hosta* 'Feather Boa'.

It was certainly a memorable experience to visit 'Towner Crest'.

The gardens of Warren Berg and June Sinclair, Port Ludlow (24April 2006)

To be in the midst of the revered rhododendron hybridist Warren Berg's garden was a rare privilege. It was thrilling to see this woodland nursery of some 2–3 acres containing his collection of exceptional hybrids and species rhododendrons, some of which were raised from seed following his plant hunting seed collections. In particular there was a truly outstanding form of *R. edgeworthii* (with five exquisite blooms per truss and having superb foliage) from the Sichuan collection 9763. An impressive hybrid *R.* 'Grenadier' × 'Rosevallon' displayed outstanding claret red indumentum and I was pleased to see *R. vaseyi* which has such pretty delicate flowers in forms of rose-pink to white and, of course, the unique prolific 'Ginny Gee'.

Tragically Warren Berg was seriously ill and unable to meet us. He died some weeks later but leaves the horticultural world with an incredible legacy of rhododendrons that perpetuate his memory.

June Sinclair, a close horticultural friend and near neighbour of Warren Berg, has a 1-acre garden with woodland conditions in a glorious waterside setting. Of note were *Rubus* 'Salmon Berry', *R. concatenans* with mustard gold blooms, and pleione orchids growing in a length of hollow tree trunk amidst a fine collection of woody ornamentals.

The Rhododendron Species Foundation, Seattle, Washington, USA (25 April 2006)

We were welcomed to the RSF by Steve Hootman, its director and a notable plant collector: he treated us to a very informative and comprehensive (if rapid) guided tour of this very extensive garden.

A comprehensive replanting programme has been undertaken since the unfortunate experiences with sawdust a few years ago, and the RSF is well on the way to becoming the definitive collection of rhododendron species. There are considerable numbers of recent introductions and a good representative selection of material introduced in the last two centuries.

Almost the first thing we saw was a collection of about 20 plants of *R. clementinae* – almost all of different provenance. Considerable progress is being made at the RSF in showing not only examples of each species, but also groups in sufficient numbers to show its variation: systematic attempts to show this variation are unusual and need to be made more often. Another interesting example was the way the differences between recent introductions of *R. wiltonii* and the older ones were demonstrated.

The RSF has taken care to provide many diverse subsections with suitable growing conditions, so the collections of both subsection Falconera and of subsection Lapponica were thriving. Many of us saw flowers on some species for the first time, for example the rarely grown *R. yungningense* and *R. websterianum* var. *websterianum*.

Especially noteworthy and new were flowering plants of *R. huianum*: its almost smoky-blue flowers and pink calyces were superb – an important addition even to that superb subsection, Fortunea. The deep yellow flowers of a Vietnam collection of *R. sinofalconeri* were also outstanding.

For sheer beauty and impact, however, the shrub of *R. pingianum* in full flower, still growing in a part of the garden that had not been replanted, was something I shall remember for a very long time. But where is the definitive collection of species in the UK?

Mike Robinson

Jim and Judy Barlup's garden; Ned Brockenbrough's garden, Bellevue WA (25 April 2006)

After leaving the Rhododendron Species Foundation, we were entertained to a wonderful lunch and sincere welcome by Jim

ROSEMARY LEGRAND

Ned Brockenbrough's garden

and Judy Barlup, following which Jim (a hybridist of outstanding rhododendrons) gave us an enthralling tour of his collection of hybrid crosses, 4000 of which were to be seen in the germination cabinets grown under full spectrum lights for 18 hours a day. He had 125 new crosses and cross-pollinates 800 crosses per year. Jim has his own seed bank with some seed from 1998 and he gave a demonstration of cross-pollination before taking us to see the stock area with an impressive range of his beautiful hybrids including *R.* 'Honey Butter'. The prolific flower, vigour and uniformity of the plants endorsed his skills.

As an appreciation of Jim and Judy's generosity to our group we presented them with a donation to Meerkerk Gardens, where Jim is acknowledged as a valued mentor.

During the afternoon we visited the gardens of another renowned rhododendron hybridist, Ned Brockenbrough. His property overlooks Lake Washington and the gardens encompass his collection of glorious rhododendron hybrids.

Looking magnificent were *R.* 'Horizon Dawn', *R.* 'Horizon Monarch' (see next page) and *R.* 'Hawk Crest' × *macabeanum.* Ned's three golden retrievers seemed as enthusiastic about the RCM group's visit as their owner.

That evening, Steve Hootman, the curator of the Rhododendron Species Botanical Garden gave us an enthralling lecture entitled 'A Year in the Life of a Plant

ROSEMARY LEGRAND

Presentation to Ned Brockenbrough

ROSEMARY LEGRAND

Rhododendron 'Horizon Monarch' at Ned Brockenbrough's garden

Hunter', relating how on an expedition in the Southern Himalayas they saw 40 species in one day. He showed us slides of a fabulous selection of exciting plants in Yunnan, Sri Lanka and Arunachal Pradesh.

Meerkerk Garden, Greenbank; Frank Fujioka's Nursery Gardens, Freeland, WA Whidbey Island (26 April 2006)

In the late 1800s the original city of Seattle was destroyed by fire. It is now an ultra-modern city, home of the amazing Space Needle. We travelled across Seattle, en route to board the Mukilteo Ferry, our destination Whidbey Island, to explore the Meerkerk Gardens.

Kristi O'Donnell met us with an interesting introduction to the gardens created by Ann and Max Meerkerk in the 1960s. Originally 13 acres, the gardens now extend to 43 acres which includes a woodland preserve. We were taken on guided tours and shown the very promising hybridising work being undertaken by their keen hybridist Oriana. The Meerkerks were particularly influenced by Exbury Gardens and also drawn to the exotic species from Asia, Max Meerkerk having lived in China. The temperate climate on the island is ideal for growing, rarely freezing at an average 30°F in winter and 70°F in summer. Ponds had to be dug to provide the water supply as the Olympic Mountains deflect most of the rainfall. Certainly the rhododendrons were flowering, *R. wasonii* with blooms of ethereal beauty proved this point as did tall purple flowered *R.* 'Whidbey Island' and the flower-laden branches of gorgeous *R. augustinii* subsp. *chasmanthum*.

A well-stocked retail nursery area displayed hybrids raised by the famous hybridists we had visited, including Frank Fujioka. Really exciting new introductions like *R.* 'Saffron Silk', a bright butter-yellow, and Jim Barlup's *R.* 'Mindy's Love', were among them. Bushy three-gallon rhododendrons were priced at $50 dollars each.

After lunch we departed for Frank Fujioka's consummate garden, a gem of a collection of superb forms of Japanese acers,

ROSEMARY LEGRAND

Kristi O'Donnell at Meerkerk Gardens

conifers such as the elegant little standard *Larix leptolepis* 'Pendula', *Prunus serrula,* and *Ulmus* 'Camperdownii' framed vistas across the multicoloured acer foliage.

My attention was drawn to a group of lovely new varieties of heuchera with delicious sounding names like 'Crème Brûlée', 'Peach Melba' and 'Key Lime Pie', which produced equally sumptuous foliage. Other memorable plants include *Acer palmatum* 'Shaina' with red foliage which makes a compact mound, Frank's hybrid *R.* 'Seaview Sunset', *Magnolia* 'Yellow Lantern', *Acer* × *conspicuum* 'Phoenix' and the curious mound forming *Dianthus freynii.* We toured the nursery and saw some of Frank's exceptional hybrids; being a very discerning breeder he has only registered 12 plants in 35 years.

Elisabeth Miller Botanical Garden, Seattle; Washington Park Arboretum, Seattle; Jim Senko's Camellia Garden, Lakewood (27 April 2006)

On a bluff above Puget Sound lies the 5-acre Elisabeth Miller Botanical Garden with spectacular views of the Sound and Olympic Peninsula. The Millers purchased the property in 1948 and Elisabeth, an ardent plantswoman, created an outstanding private collection of rare and choice plants. During her lifetime she supported and inspired many horticultural organisations. In turn she received numerous accolades. It is no surprise that enthusiasts are eager to visit this garden in which there are over 4,500 living taxa, comprising ericaceous plants, ferns, grasses and alpines, all benefiting from the micro climate.

The Great Plant Picks Educational Programme was launched by the garden in 2000 to form a comprehensive list of selected plants suited to the Pacific Northwest. It is based on the RHS awards system.

Currently the garden is foremost in collecting and breeding hepatica species and cultivars. It also holds an enviable group of epimedium in variety, in particular *Epimedium grandiflorum* var. *higoense* 'Bandit', *E.* × *youngianium* 'Be my Valentine' and *E.* × *omeiense*, many selected and introduced by Darrell R Probst of Garden Vision Nursery, Massachusetts USA. Other plants of interest include *Anemonella thalictroides rubra plena*, *Dryopteris polylepis* with a striking black crown and stipes, the bizarre *Hosta* 'White Feather', completely white but second leaf growth in green with a white fleck, a stunningly beautiful copper-orange grass *Restio tetraphyllus* for dry temperate areas, and finally a gorgeous *R. johnstoneanum* 'Double Diamond'.

Elisabeth Miller was a regular customer of Hilliers, and requested they send anything new to her, no doubt a factor in the creation of such a marvellous plant collection.

Unfortunately time did not permit more than a most enlightening introduction and brief coach drive through Washington Park Arboretum, which is the second largest arboretum in the world, covering 230 acres, with the largest collection of Champion Trees in the United States, among them 17 different magnolia varieties.

In the list of endangered plants, five species of magnolias and three of rhododendrons, including *R. degronianum* subsp. *yakushimanum,* are grown. The Arboretum contains over 5,500 different kinds of plants and trees, collections include a three-quarter mile walk lined with flowering prunus, azaleas and cornus. They have a 'Loderi Valley' of hybrids and large leaved rhododendrons, sheltered by magnolias, and a 'Rhododendron Glen', south of which is part of the camellia collection covering 2.5 acres. This collection was assembled from the late 1930s onwards, it contains many older cultivars and hybrids, some of which are very rare.

The Elisabeth Miller Library, the most important horticultural library in the Pacific Northwest, and the Otis Douglas Hyde Herbarium, which is probably the nation's largest collection of preserved cultivated plants, are within the Arboretum.

We crossed into the state of Oregon to visit Jim Senko's camellia garden at Lakewood Park. After retiring from the nursery trade, Jim and Pat purchased 3.3 acres in 1995 and have created a haven of choice plants and wildlife with the accent on camellias, which were looking at their best. Some are trained on wooden structures in full sun and others are in dappled shade. I was very impressed with *C.* 'Silver Triumph', a white semi-double Nuccio hybrid, also of interest were *C.* 'Mabel Bryant' and the deeply serrated foliage of *C.* 'Holly Bright'. Jim has 45 varieties of sasanqua including a form named 'Feathers Fragrant'. All the plants were flourishing at Lakewood.

En route to Portland, long drifts of blue camassia growing alongside the freeway as we passed Olympia were an eye-catching sight. We marvelled at the majestic distant snow-covered peaks of Mt Baker, Mt Hood, Mt St Helens and Mt Rainier, which is the third tallest mountain in the USA at 14,411ft. It is still an active volcano.

Bishops Close, Elk Rock Garden; The Susan Bates Garden; Crystal Springs Rhododendron Garden; Van Veen Nursery; Portland (28 April 2006)

After arriving the previous evening at Portland, it was very noticeable to see the number of fine specimens of *Cornus florida* planted in private gardens and around municipal buildings. Portland is famous for its Rose Festival held in June and its classical Chinese and Japanese Gardens. It is also one of the foremost regions of the US for large-scale growers of nursery stock, there being 180 nurseries from Portland to Salem.

Morning dew was still visible on the sweeping lawns of the Elk Rock Garden created by Peter Kerr, a Scotsman who came to Portland in 1888 and started a grain business. This peaceful oasis of 13 acres has a splendid array of choice plants and trees, fine specimens of stewartia, parrotia and a huge *Magnolia grandiflora*. We saw a shrubby form of *Arctostaphylos menziesii* and the brilliant pink flowers of *Loropetalum chinense* 'Pipa's Red', together with the exciting *Sinocalycanthus chinensis* and a beautiful display of *Daphne genkwa* in bloom.

Elk Rock was the childhood home and garden of Anne Kerr MacDonald and her sister Jane Kerr Platt, who had several plants named after her including *M. stellata* 'Jane Platt' which is said to be superior to *M.* 'Leonard Messel'.

The former home and garden of Lady McDonald is now owned by Susan Bates who graciously gave us a tour of her garden, with awesome views of Mt Hood. A perfect specimen of *Metasequoia glyptostroboides* was to be admired as well as *Rehderodendron macrocarpum* in full bloom and the lovely *R. prinophyllum* 'Marie Hoffman'.

Arriving at Crystal Springs Rhododendron Garden we were entertained to a sumptuous lunch by the Portland Chapter of the American Rhododendron Society in the glorious 7-acre surroundings. The garden was jointly established in 1950 by Portland Parks and the Portland Chapter and is maintained by volunteers. Franklinia, stewartia and davidia thrive along with 1500 to 2000 rhododendrons and azaleas. After a speech of thanks and presentations, by Mike Robinson, we explored the gardens that circle the spring-fed lake and admired the colourful visual picture. The generous friendship afforded us on this occasion will not be forgotten.

Vicki Molina, who had joined us for lunch, then welcomed us to the famous Van Veen 4-acre nursery. Kathy Van Veen is the third generation of expert propagators of azaleas and rhododendrons. Her grandfather Theodore emigrated from the Netherlands 100 years ago. He invented the mist propagation system and heated cables for benches. The nursery, which he started in 1926 now grows a truly great selection of varieties including a superb range of maddenias and vireyas. The tour of the nursery was absorbing, showing the emphasis on the use of recycled materials. They obtain excellent propagation results and will root cuttings to order using traditional methods.

The Jane Platt Garden, Portland; Jenkins Estate, Aloha; Cooper Mountain Vineyards, Beaverton, Oregon. (29 April 2006)

David Platt afforded us the rare privilege of visiting his late mother's wonderful garden which extends to over 5 acres, 2.5 of which are in formal landscape and mostly laid out in the 1960s.

Clearly evident is the artistic flair that Jane Platt brought to her garden design, particularly in the rock garden, within which you find a formidable collection of choice plants including a wonderful, compact white trillium with anemone centre. Fine specimen trees include a mature *Davidia involucrata* which has a variegated south-facing side, plants from which are named after Jane Platt.

We arrived at the 68-acre Jenkins Estate as the guests of the Tualatin Valley Chapter, not only to see their exceptionally good ARS Spring Show, but also to be entertained to a delectable lunch prepared by the members. It was a great opportunity to meet them and learn about their Chapter and exhibitors. The Chapter invited John Rawling to be a judge at the show. In the surrounding 5 acres of gardens are planted 400 azaleas and rhododendrons.

The Spring Show exhibited a large range of rhododendrons in variety with superb trusses (*R.* 'Tahitian Dawn' and *R.* 'Red Olympia' were two stunning examples), some of which were raised in Oregon.

On our return journey the group visited Cooper Mountain Vineyards for a wine tasting, which no doubt refreshed some weary rhododendron enthusiasts.

Gossler Farms Nursery; Springfield Northwest Garden Nursery, Eugene, Oregon (30th April 2006)

An amazing morning was spent with Roger, Marj and Eric Gossler at their exciting nursery, the catalogue for which is brimming with a wonderful selection of choice plants and trees, among them a peach coloured *Magnolia* 'Woodsman' and *Fothergilla* 'Jane Platt'. They generously allowed us to view the nursery stock in their growing tunnels where we saw a truly outstanding *Davidia involucrata* 'Sonoma', which produces some bracts up to 8in long on grafted one–two-year-old trees, and *Quercus dentata* 'Carl Ferris Miller' named after the famous South Korean gardener. *Cornus kousa* 'Wolf Eyes' and 'Summer Fun' were as gorgeous as *C. mas* 'Variegata' and beautiful *Enkianthus campanulatus* 'Variegatus', while *Daphne* 'Briggs Moonlight' had eye-catching variegated foliage. But these were surpassed by the stunning *Acer pseudoplatanus* 'Eskimo Sunset' which with *Davidia* 'Sonoma' created major plant lust amongst the group.

Next on our itinerary was the Northwest garden nursery of Marietta and Ernie O'Byrne's – a charismatic example of complementary plant associations showing a beautiful combination of colour and texture with rare and choice plants for all garden conditions. *Podophyllum delavayi* and *Brunnera* 'Looking Glass', a superb hybrid of *B.* 'Jack Frost', were in a shady bed planted with trilliums, *Arisaema taiwanense* and *A. candidissimum*. All these and so many more treasures were growing in the small nursery, like *Podophyllum pleianthum* (the Chinese Mayapple). We deeply regretted not being able to purchase plants from Gossler Farm and Northwest Nurseries.

On our last evening in Portland a presentation of special rhododendrons was made to Charlie Sale in appreciation of his enormous contribution to making the tour such a triumph.

Strybing Arboretum, San Francisco, California (1 May 2006)

Farewells were exchanged as Charlie returned to Vancouver and we flew down to San Francisco with an afternoon's visit to Strybing Arboretum. Here we saw handsome specimen trees, Australasian and South African plants, banksias in flower, silver leaved Leucadendron and the huge *Geranium maderense*. Personally, the highlight was the garden of Californian native plants – a wild flower meadow with a fusion of brilliant colours from the poppies and Pacific iris. Before we left we visited the nearby Japanese Garden.

Quarryhill Botanical Garden (2 May 2006)

Travelling along the freeway to Quarryhill we passed expansive plantings of blossom laden *Rosa banksiae* 'Lutea' along the boundaries of the various vineyards where the roses are used as mildew monitors.

Quarryhill (in the Valley of the Moon) is an extensive 61 acres containing a 20-acre cultivated garden devoted to advance the conservation, study and cultivation of the temperate flora of Asia, created originally in 1968 by Jane Davenport Jansen.

Greeted by the curator, Carol Brandt, we were taken to see an incredible collection of species trees and plants. We passed *Emmenopterys henryi*, *Idesia polycarpa* with its bunches of orange berries and *Staphylea bumalda*, as we descended to the quarry waterfalls and ponds around which grew *Rosa banksiae*. We noted *Pterostyrax hispida*, *Acer tataricum*, and *A. fulvescens*, also Magnolias *wilsonii, denudata* and *hypoleuca* (*M. obovata* Thunb.). Climbing to the viewpoint to admire the rocky panorama in rattlesnake country framed by the poignant prayer flags and *Malus sikkimensis*, we felt like inveterate plant hunters particularly passing the extravagant bunches of bright green leaves on rare *Pinus roxburghii*. At Quarryhill they have 20 different michelias and so many more treasures. After a glimpse of enchanting *Rosa chinesis* var. *spontanea,* it seemed a tragedy to leave.

Returning, we saw the awesome spectacle of the Golden Gate Bridge which has over 80,000 miles of steel wire making up the two main cables – enough to circle the world three times.

Filoli Mansion (3 May 2006)

Starting our final day on a high note, Jackie Coggan from Arena Travel, our exceptional Tour Manager, had arranged for us to visit Filoli mansion and the 16 acres of formal gardens created mostly by Mrs Lurline B. Roth. The design of the mansion was based on Muckross Park in southern Ireland and originally built by Mr Bourne who purchased Muckross for his daughter on her marriage.

Bathed in glorious sunshine, the gardens were alive with vibrant coloured tulips. *Rosa banksiae* 'Lutea' and *Clematis armandii* were in bloom, with the largest dark purple racemes of *Wisteria sinensis* 'Black Dragon' that I have ever seen.

We left the haunting beauty of Filoli to make our departure from the USA knowing that our generous friends 'across the pond' did us proud. It was indeed a phenomenal trip.

Rosemary Legrand is a horticultural speaker on gardens, a former nursery owner and daughter of George Hyde, the azalea and rhododendron hybridist. She is a member of the Group

Main Rhododendron Competition 2007

The 2007 RHS Main Rhododendron Competition will be held at Rosemoor on Saturday and Sunday April 21 and 22. This is after three successful years at Borde Hill, and is in line with RHS policy to move the Show around the country. The SW Branch is assisting the Shows Dept and Rosemoor with the organisation, and Alun Edwards, although standing down as Branch Chairman in October 2006, will coordinate this assistance.

It is the intention of the SW Branch that there will be both a Camellia and Magnolia event, at the same time, details of which will be distributed later.

Please put these dates in your diary.It is hoped that maximum support will be given to the event by all our Membership, and that members living in the southwest, in particular, will support it with a large number of entries.

Competitions

Rhododendron arboreum subsp. *delavayi* var. *peramoenum*. Part of the Tregothnan entry that took first place in Class 1 at the Early Rhododendron Competition

The Early Rhododendron Competition
Vincent Square, Westminster
March 14–15 2006

If it wasn't for the commendable efforts of The Hon. E.A.H. Boscawen and those from his Cornish garden of Tregothnan, the Early Rhododendron Competition would have been yet another embarrassment and yet another dismal attempt at promoting rhododendrons in an era when it is most required. There is no doubt that, in showing blooms in over half of the 22 classes, Tregothnan saved the day and in doing so brought a precious touch of spring to a winter that had dragged on for far too long. For their endeavours, they were awarded the Alan Hardy Challenge Salver, presented for winning more first, second and third prizes than any other competitor – in their case, easily!

The only other entrants to come away with anything were Chris Fairweather and Brian Wright.

Chris again produced a spectacular array of vireyas. He won both of the Competition's 'tender' classes. In that for trusses, he placed six entries and was awarded first prize for 'Bold Janus', a sort of pale orange or apricot flowerer with handsome, deep green leaves. 'Java Light', with luminous orange/red blooms, took second prize while the yellow* species *Rhododendron zoelleri* from Papua New Guinea claimed third prize.

In the class for sprays he was first with 'Tropic Fanfare', a dainty yellow/orange flowered exhibit, and second with 'Saxon Glow' – salmon corollas perched on unusually long stems. Brian Wright achieved first and third prizes for two small-leaved sprays. Respectively, these were the *R. leucaspis* hybrid 'Bric-a-Brac' and the popular 'Cilpinense'.

Outstanding among the Tregothnan entries were those shown in the following classes:

Class 1 for trusses of three different species. Here, for first prize, they staged *R. macabeanum*, *R. arboreum* subsp. *delavayi* var. *peramoenum* (see facing page) and *R. siderophyllum.* Although impressive, the Grandia specimen was not the best of the Tregothnan macabes which are well-worth seeing if you're in that neck of the woods in early spring. For the cognoscenti, *R. delavayi* var. *peramoenum* must have been a treat but, for my money, not in the same league as its broader leaved, bigger flowered relative, *R. delavayi* var. *delavayi. R. siderophyllum,* being of the Triflora persuasion, was altogether different from its two companions but quite pretty with its dense cluster of white flowers and greyish/green leaves.

Class 7 for any Fortunea truss featured *R. praevernum* which received only second prize; perhaps for being not as pert as it might have been.

Class 10 for 'dwarf' species. In this class Tregothnan were awarded first, second and third prizes for a nice *R. dauricum* (quite late for Cornwall) their pretty *R. siderophyllum* and good *R. scabrifolium* which I think was var. *spiciferum*.

Class 15 for any hybrid truss. Here, they showed an excellent but unnamed *R. barbatum* creation. The other parent was unknown but it was every bit as good as a decent form of its named parent. It was rightly given first prize.

Although rhododendrons are no longer the gardening force that they once were – and this competition, with only Tregothnan to uphold it, went some way to underline this – it might improve matters somewhat if this event was held a week or two later than the middle of March. I know that this idea has been discussed by the Shows Committee but nothing seems to have been done. A later competition would probably coincide with more plants in bloom which hopefully would encourage more gardens, with more blooms, to take part. It seems that there would be nothing to lose, unless hall bookings for other purposes absolutely prevent this.

Brian Wright

*As a plant producing bi-coloured blooms, *R. zoelleri* flowers can also be orange.

The Main Rhododendron Competition
Borde Hill Garden Sussex
22–23 April 2006
Species

This show was a great success, helped by lovely weather on the first day. A show which gave pleasure not only to rhododendron, camellia and magnolia enthusiasts, but also to the many visitors, some of whom we hope, may be converted to these elite groups of plants.

The competition was very keen, and nearly all the classes were well supported, with a high standard of well staged exhibits – which gave the judges quite a challenge.

Our hosts, Borde Hill, set a high standard, exhibiting a very fine truss of *R. sinogrande* in Class 3 – to gain first, against the stiff competition of ten entries. They also gained first place in Class 8 with *R. montroseanum*, a class of fifteen entries!

A superb *R. arboreum* subsp. *cinnamomeum* var. *roseum,* well staged by P Holmes in Class 5 gained first prize for Nymans. Brian Wright also won first prize in Class 11 with a particularly fine specimen of *R. lacteum.*

The winners in each class were:

Class 1 (six species). Six entries for The Lionel de Rothschild Challenge Cup: Borde Hill for *R. anthosphaerum*, *R. falconeri* subsp. *eximium, R. rex* subsp. *fictolacteum, R. fulvum, R. arboreum* and *R. morii*

Class 2 (three species). Seven entries: Nymans for *R. thomsonii, R. oreodoxa* and *R. denudatum*

Class 3 (any species). Ten entries for The McLaren Challenge Cup: Borde Hill for *R. sinogrande* (see facing page)

Class 4 (any species). Nine entries: Nymans for *R. wardii* KW5736

Class 5 (Arborea, Argyrophylla). Ten entries: Nymans Garden for *R. arboreum* subsp. *cinnamomeum* var. *roseum* (see facing page)

Class 6 (Barbata, Glischra, Maculifera). Seven entries: Exbury for *R. pachysanthum*

Class 7 (Campanulata, Fulgensia, Lanata).

MICHAEL SHUTTLEWORTH

Rhododendron montroseanum which won a first place in Class 8 for Borde Hill Garden

Six entries: R White (Second prize) for *R. campanulatum*
Class 8 (Grandia, Falconera). 15 entries: Borde Hill for *R. montroseanum* (see below)
Class 9 (Fortunea). Seven entries: Borde Hill for *R. sutchuenense*
Class 10 (Fulva, Irrorata, Parishia). 11 entries: Borde Hill for *R. irroratum* 'Polka Dot'
Class 11 (Taliensia). 20 entries: B Wright for *R. lacteum*
Class 12 (Neriiflora). Ten entries: Nymans for *R. sperabile* var. *weihsiense*
Class 13 (Pontica). Six entries: R White for *R. hyperythrum*
Class 14 (Thomsonia, Selensia, Campylocarpa). Eight entries: Nymans for *R. wardii*
Class 15 & 16 No entries
Class 17 (Edgeworthia, Maddenia). Two entries: High Beeches for *R. ciliatum*
Class 18 No Entries
Class 19 (Triflora, Heliolepida). Six entries: Nymans for *R. siderophyllum*
Class 20 (*R. augustinii*). Two entries: Nymans
Class 21 (Cinnabarina, Tephropepla, Virgata). One entry: Nymans (second prize) for *R. cinnabarinum* subsp. *xanthocodon*
Class 22 (Campylogyna, Genestieriana, Glauca). Three entries: Nymans for *R. prunifolium*
Class 23 (Lapponica). Eight entries: Borde Hill for *R. hippophaeoides*
Class 24 (Saluenensia, Uniflora). One entry: R White for *R. pemakoense*
Class 25 (Scabrifolia). Six entries: Borde Hill for *R. racemosum*
Class 26 (Pogonanthum, Lepidota). Four entries: R White for *R. primuliflorum cephalanthoides*
Class 27 (Any other Lepidote species): Two entries: R White for *R. megeratum*

MICHAEL SHUTTLEWORTH

Rhododendron sinogrande that won first place for Borde Hill Garden in Class 3

MICHAEL SHUTTLEWORTH

Rhododendron arboreum subsp. *cinnamomeum* var. *roseum* took first place for Nymans Garden in Class 5

Class 28 No entries
Class 29 (Deciduous Azaleas). One entry; Exbury for *R. reticulatum*
Class 30 No entries

May I conclude this report by saying how much exhibitors, stewards and judges appreciate the guidance of Dr David Chamberlain, who for so many years has been of help with regard to nomenclature of species.

Archie Skinner

Main Rhododendron Competition
Hybrids

This was the third year running that the Main Rhododendron Competition has been held at Borde Hill. Until Borde Hill, this competition had been always held in the RHS halls at Vincent Square but was, for some years, sadly in decline. There was no doubt that the decision to leave London breathed new life into the event, especially since it was so enthusiastically welcomed by Borde Hill and so well supported – by the Shows Department of the RHS; the ICS with their camellia competition; the SE Branch of the RCM Group with their organisational work, stewarding and magnolia competition; the sponsors viz. Loder Plants, Starborough Nurseries and The High Beeches; the various trade stands, many of whom displayed plants of great quality and interest; and the non-competitive displays that were both attractive and informative.

In 2007 the Competition moves on to Rosemoor and if it is half as successful there as it has been at Borde Hill, it will be an event well-worth attending and taking part in.

But to the Hybrids Section of the 2006 Competition. This consisted of 26 classes and, probably for the first time ever wasn't dominated by any of the major gardens. In fact it was the far more modest Crowborough garden of Kilsaran, owned by Brian Wright, which bagged more prizes than any other. One might say, about time, since Brian had been trying for over 30 years to achieve such a dubious honour. Anyhow, his effort wasn't quite good enough to include some silverware. This went to Leonardslee who won the Loder Cup for showing the Competition's best hybrid truss and, in effect, took the trophy back home. The entry responsible for this was a fine unnamed cross between *R. hodgsonii* and *R. falconeri*. So congratulations to Tom Loder and his right-hand man Andy Stevens.

The Crosfield Challenge Cup, for three hybrids raised in the garden of the exhibitor, went, yet again, to Exbury. Their name has been engraved on this cup so many times that one feels it should have a permanent place in their trophy cabinet. To win it this year, they showed the worthy, big-leaved 'Fortune', 'Lionel's Triumph' and 'Quaker Girl', a Rothschild cross made over 50 years ago between *R. hyperythrum* and 'Avalanche'. With large, white spotted green corollas it showed great poise and, for me, was the best hybrid in the show.

But close behind must have been 'Kalimna' from the same garden. This was shown as one of Exbury's six in the six-truss class. It was from a cross between 'Edith Boulter' and 'Unknown Warrior'. Pale rose with a yellowish brown tone, it was also influenced by *R. campylocarpum* and *R. griffithianum* blood.

Other eye-catching entries were the prizewinners in the large spray class viz. a Borde Hill *campylocarpum* hybrid labelled

'East Lodge Form' which won first prize, a *campylocarpum* × *fortunei* from The High Beeches which took second prize (see right) and the better known 'Eleanore' (*rubiginosum* × *augustinii*) from Exbury which was awarded third prize.

In the class for exhibits with subsect. Arborea or Argyrophylla parentage, Exbury showed a splendid truss of 'Endeavour'. A cross between *R. arboreum cinnamomeum* var. *album* and *R. lacteum*, this boasted rich creamy flowers with purplish spots and foliage with an attractive silvery brown indumentum. The judges had no hesitation in awarding this first prize.

MICHAEL SHUTTLEWORTH

Rhododendron campylocarpum x *fortunei*.
Exhibited by The High Beeches

In one of the lepidote classes first prize was awarded to Brian Wright for a pretty vase of 'Pematit Cambridge', an obviously named pale blue derived from *pemakoense* × 'Blue Tit'. Just as pretty was the runner-up, a lovely lilac pink spray of 'Emasculum' (*ciliatum* × *dauricum*) shown by John Lancaster of Balcombe Forest, Sussex.

Chris Fairweather again paraded an outstanding collection of vireyas and deservedly won six prizes. Among them were 'Golden Girl' (a strong yellow) 'Shantung Rose', (too seedy a name for a most elegant pink/vermilion flower) 'Captain Scarlet', 'Jiminy Cricket' and 'Pink Ray', an enchanting pastel pink.

Smaller Garden Classes: in addition to the main species and hybrid classes, there are now four classes for those with gardens of less than three acres. Those eligible for this section of the Competition are not precluded from entering any other class, which does give those who garden on a smaller basis more opportunity of becoming prize-winners.

All the prizes in this year's section seemed to be won by Barry Haseltine and Brian Wright. Among his various exhibits, Barry showed two particularly good sprays of *R. racemosum* and *R. davidsonianum* while

Brian Wright's Tower Court form *R. lacteum* might have been regarded as his most notable, especially since it also claimed a prize or two in the main species section. Mind you, this was its first spring flowering in 27 years (it had previously poorly flowered only in October; possibly a *lacteum* trait), so perhaps it was worth a prize just for the wait.

Brian Wright

Early Camellia Competition
Vincent Square
14–15 March 2006

Just like the Early Rhododendron Competition held a bench or two away, the Camellia set-to was also dominated by one major garden – The Chatsworth House Trust; an historic garden indeed but also famous for its glass, particularly where camellias are concerned.

This year, out of 24 classes, the Chatsworth name appeared on no less than 28 prize-cards. Broken down, this amounted to 15 first prizes, seven second prizes and six third prizes. Indeed, there was not a lot left for any of the other entrants to win but Jill Totty did get the better of Chatsworth twice with winning entries. The first of these was for three single flowered japonicas. Here she showed a trio of very good reds viz. 'Bright Buoy', a Les Jury hybrid with golden anthers and dark green leaves; 'Ludgvan's Red', more properly known without the apostrophe 's'; and 'Midnight Serenade', a brilliant dark red originated by Nuccio's. The second was for any semi-double japonica. Here she succeeded with yet another fine red – 'San Dimas'. This was an impressively large bloom probably 12cm or more in diameter.

MICHAEL SHUTTLEWORTH

Camellia 'El Dorado'.
Winner of two first prizes.
Exhibited by The Chatsworth House Trust

MICHAEL SHUTTLEWORTH

Camellia 'Dona Herzilia de Freitas Magalhaes'.
Exhibited by The Chatsworth House Trust

Alan Smith was the only other contestant to win against the great garden. He outdid them in the class for any three semi-double japonicas where he showed two superb reds, 'Bob Hope' and 'Grand Prix', alongside the glowing white 'Lovelight'. Grown under glass and plainly cultivated for showing, these were huge blooms as big, one might say, as many large retics.

As for Chatsworth, they gave us far too many good things for all to be recorded here but among their more outstanding prize-winners were:

Any six japonica cultivars: In this class, they won with a top notch entry of 'Adolphe Audusson', 'Drama Girl' (a very dramatic salmon pink) 'Guilio Nuccio' (a most attractive two-tone coral pink) 'Latifolia' (ancient but still a fine camellia) 'Mathotiana' (a massive ruby coloured exhibit) and 'R.L.Wheeler'.

Any three japonicas: Here, they won with 'Bob Hope', 'Margaret Davis' and 'Mrs. D. W. Davis'.

Any single flowered japonica: 'Jupiter' – galactic in light red with white stripes – was bold in bloom, faultless in condition and unquestionably worth first place.

Any anemone or peony-formed japonica: Here, Chatsworth won with 'Powder Puff', apparently a commercial synonym for a very old variety called 'Souvenir de Madame Colette van Wassenhove'. On the other hand, I'm not sure whether it's more accurately a seedling of the less pithily named plant. Whatever, it was bride white and so good that you could almost see the powder rising from its delicate petals and masses of petaloids.

Mention should also be made of a stunning 'Francie L' and a cereal-bowl sized 'Harold L. Paige' which both came out on top in each of the two retic classes.

The soft pink 'El Dorado' was also noteworthy (see facing page). This peony formed beauty picked-up first prize in two classes.

Although I earlier referred to 'Mathotiana' often known as 'Mathotiana Rubra', I did not say how utterly impressed I was with this 'must have' plant particularly if you are able to grow it under glass. In this year's competition its blooms won three first prizes and in previous years many more. It was raised by M. Mathot of Ghent way back in 1847 or thereabouts. The flower is not only strikingly large under glass but formal and beautifully formed with dark red imbricated petals. And, as an added bonus, it is usually long-lasting on the bush.

Brian Wright

Main Camellia Competition
Vincent Square
11-12 April 2006

The cool early weather conditions continued between the early and main Camellia competitions, slowing the season dramatically in some areas of the country. This was compounded by snow in the two days before the show with up to 8 inches falling in some areas. These wintry conditions amplified the differences between the glasshouse grown and blooms produced without protection. Indeed the often criticized situation of plants being judged equally when grown under these different conditions did not appear to be such a significant issue this year as without the greenhouse produced blooms the show would have been sparse indeed, with many classes consisting of no or very few entries. Judging appeared to be highly consistent this year, with no major errors, for which the stewards should be commended.

Classes 1 through 5 of the Competition make up Division 1 and call for camellia sprays displayed in the familiar RHS vases.

Class 1 attracted just a single entry. Mrs B Griffiths of Thames Ditton should be commended for her efforts in achieving a second place for three vases containing sprays from 'Debbie', 'Thelma Dale', and an unknown variety.

Class 3 was won by Ms D Choa from London with surely the best spray of camellias seen at a London show for many years. The vase of the white formal double 'Nuccio's Gem' was virtually unmarked and of the highest quality. Second was awarded to Brian Wright with an almost equally fine vase of 'Scented Red', and third was Mrs Griffiths with 'Lavinia Maggi'.

Class 4 went to Brian Wright with a spray of 'Debbie' consisting of no less than ten open blooms and several breaking buds. Brian was also second with 'Mary Christian'. In Class 5 Brian Wright was awarded second place with 'Inspiration' with the pinkest of pink flowers, First was awarded to Mrs Griffiths with 'Spring Festival'.

Division 2 of the Competition is for the more familiar cut blooms displayed in cups and is made up of Classes 10 – 27.

Class 10 went again to Warwickshire's David Davis, continuing several years success in this class for the Leonardslee Bowl. Requiring 12 blooms, David won with a very fresh set including 'Tiffany', 'Dr Clifford Parks', 'Lasca Beauty', 'Onetia Holland', 'Guilio Nuccio', 'Lovelight', 'Owen Henry', 'Elegans Champagne', 'Elegans Splendor', 'Desire', 'Margaret Davis' and 'Kitty Berry'. Andy Simons from Bedfordshire came second and third (as he did last year) with his second place set dominated by reticulatas including 'Interval', 'Pavlova' (see p.106), 'Hulyn Smith', and 'Lasca Beauty'. Fourth place was awarded to Jill Totty from Fordingbridge whose 12 included two blooms in 'Bob Hope' and 'San Dimas' which demonstrated the deepest reds in the show. It should be noted that although 'Bob Hope' gives fine reds, the blooms in the UK rarely exhibit a clean semi-double form but are somewhat spoiled by occasional extra petals.

Class 11 requiring six different blooms went this year to Andy Simons with a group of small and miniature blooms concentrating on colour variations 'Kakureiso', 'Lemon Drop', 'Ave Maria', 'Takanini', 'Black Opal' and 'Cupcake'. Hampshire's Exbury Gardens came second with 'Bob Hope', again showing well, Mrs B Griffiths was third, with fourth going to Alan Smith of Swanage whose six contained an outstanding 'Anticipation'.

Class 12 for any three single flowers was won by Andy Simons with a group including 'Quercifolia' – as the name suggests, the foliage of this plant is reminiscent of an evergreen oak. Second place went to Nick Creek of Ardingly with three plants of his own creation, an achievement for which Nick should be justly proud. The three plants were 'Brown Creeks Charm', 'Lustre', and 'Twilight'. Hybridisation of camellias in the UK is at almost a standstill with few new varieties registered each year and of these a very low percentage have strong enough characteristics to succeed commercially. In order to encourage some more focused hybridising it may be appropriate for the RHS Show Schedule Committee to introduce a class or two specifically for 'home' produced hybrids. Such classes should be rewarded to a higher degree than other classes to specifically encourage the hybridiser; (possibly the RCM group) could be involved in sponsoring these classes.

Class 13 for a single-flowered bloom was well won by Brian Wright with an exceptional example of 'Scented Red', regrettably, as with so many 'scented' Japonicas, my nose could not detect any fragrance on a cool London morning. Second went to Nick Creek with another of his own creation, 'Brown Creeks Rosary'; third was Jill Totty with 'Bright Buoy'.

Class 14 for any three semi-double japonicas was taken by David Davis with a fine collection of 'Guilio Nuccio', 'Lovelight' and 'Bob Hope'. Second was Andy Simons whose three included the unusual bowl shaped bloom 'Hana Fuki'; Jill Totty was third.

Class 15 for any one semi-double japonica was won by Andy Simons with 'Lovelight'. It is interesting how a specific variety can have a good year across the whole country; it was obviously that good year for 'Lovelight' as a number of exceptional blooms of this variety appeared throughout this show. Alan Smith was second with an enormous bloom of 'Grand Prix' and Mrs MA Pelton was third with 'Berenice Boddy'.

Class 16 for any three anemone- or peony-form japonicas was won by Andy Simons with 'Mark Allan', 'Easter Morn' and 'Takanini'. Unlike many commercial camellias, Takanini seems to improve with age, with the blooms becoming larger with even greater depth of colour as the plant matures, It should really be grown much more widely. Jill Totty came second with 'Marina', 'Kick Off' and 'Elegans'. David Davis was very unfortunate to come only third with a fine grouping of 'Elegans Splendor', 'Onetia Holland' and 'Tiffany'. Exbury achieved fourth place.

MICHAEL SHUTTLEWORTH

Camellia 'Nuccio's Ruby'. Part of David Davis' prize-winning entry for Class 20

Class 17 is for any one anemone or peony form. David Davis just got the nod over Alan Smith with David's 'Tiffany' overcoming Alan's 'Dixie Night'. Alan also achieved third with 'Blaze of Glory'.

Class 18 for any three formal doubles went to David Davis with 'Desire', 'Nuccio's Pearl' and 'Nuccio's Gem'. Nick Creek was second with 'Mrs Tingley', 'Kay Truesdale' and 'Desire', while third was Jill Totty with a set including the excellent 'Willamina'.

Class 19 called for a single bloom of a formal double japonica. First was Andy Simons with a typically large 'Augusto Pinto', Second was Jill Totty with 'C M Hovey', third was Ms D Chou with 'Nuccio's Gem'.

Class 20 is an area that causes a small amount of confusion among some competitors as it calls for any three hybrids. This normally produces a rather uneven contest between the showy reticulata hybrids, the *C.* × *williamsii* group, and the more unusual crosses. David Davis was successful with a three of 'Lasca Beauty', 'Dr Clifford

MICHAEL SHUTTLEWORTH

Camellia 'Pavlova'. Part of Andy Simons' second place set in Class 10

Parks' and 'Nuccio's Ruby' (see previous page). 'Nuccio's Ruby' is probably the richest red of any of the reticulatas but normally the papery petals are prone to folding damage in the bud and the blooms generally lack substance, but this was certainly not the case with the flower in this competition, as David managed to produce the best example I have ever seen at home or abroad, including examples in California. Second was Andy Simons, with three very large blooms of 'Lasca Beauty', 'Jean Pursel' and 'Hulyn Smith'; Brian Wright was third with 'Mary Christian', 'Inspiration' and 'Donation'.

In Class 21 for any one hybrid Andy Simons came first and second with 'Jean Pursel' and 'Hulyn Smith'. Brian Wright was third with 'Inspiration'.

Class 22 calls for any three *C.* × *williamsii* hybrids. Andy Simons won with 'Joyful Bells', an unknown variety, and 'Muskoka'. Jill Totty was placed second with 'Brigadoon', 'Mirage' and 'Anticipation'. It appears the judges did get this wrong, as Jill's three did appear significantly fresher. Andy Simons was third with 'Cupcake', 'Elsie Jury', and 'Debbie'.

Andy Simons completed a clean sweep in Class 23 for any one single-flowered hybrid. The winning bloom was 'Cupcake' – a relatively new Nuccio introduction that is predominantly white with pink shading; with × *williamsii* characteristics it appears to be very suited to UK gardens and should be grown more widely.

Class 21 for any semi-double hybrid was won by Alan Smith with 'Carolyn Williams', Nick Creek was second and third with 'Brigadoon' and 'Daintiness'.

Class 22 for any peony-form hybrid usually turns into a competition between which Jury hybrid will win, and this year Andy Simons came first and second with 'Elsie Jury' and the Felix Jury form of 'Debbie', Alan Smith came third with the normal 'Debbie'. It appears to me that the Felix Jury form more correctly known as 'Debbie's Carnation' is a much deeper colour than the normal variety and blooms significantly earlier.

As mentioned earlier, in some years a particular plant will succeed across the whole country, and following this theme we saw in Class 26 that an entire group of plants had not appreciated this year's weather conditions. Requiring a formal double × *williamsii,* the competition drew only two entries, both of 'Waterlily'. Neither bloom had quite the quality to merit a first place Consequently second was awarded to Nick Creek and third to Jill Totty.

Class 27 can be absolutely fascinating as it allows us to see the diversity in the Camellia world. This class calls for any hybrid or species not covered elsewhere in the competition. Andy Simons won with *C. glabsipetala,* a large flowered single species with wavy petals, flowers open shell-pink and fade to white. Andy was also second with 'Honeymoon', a hybrid containing the yellow species *C. nitidissima* – the yellow shows at the base of each petal. Third place was taken by Jill Totty with the excellent small flowered *C. transnokoensis* a plant that is defying expectation and proving hardy across most of the southern counties and beyond.

Class 28 is a recently introduced class requiring an arrangement of camellias. This was won by Mrs H Keates of Kingston-upon-Thames with an even and compact vase of 'Miss Charleston Covina', second was Andy Simons with a vase containing a mix of several small leaved species.

Andy Simons

Southeast Branch Magnolia Competition
Borde Hill Garden
22–23 April 2006

One of the latest springs for many a year did not bode well for the Main RHS Show at Borde Hill on 22 and 23 April, but, on the weekend, gardeners came up with enough superb flowers to make another fine spectacle for the public visiting the show – part of the Spring Plant Fair held at Borde Hill. Sponsorship to help defray the costs of running the event came from Loder Plants, Starborough and Reuthe Nurseries and The High Beeches garden. The South East Branch of the Rhododendron, Camellia and Magnolia Group was responsible for the Magnolia Competition, held in the large marquee put up for the Spring Fair; ten classes covered the full range of possible entries, with two of the classes specifically restricted to flowers from gardens of under 3 acres. The weather took its toll on two classes, for which there were no entries at all, and one other where only one spray appeared.

Eight gardens entered, with the home garden of Borde Hill and that of Maurice Foster dominating, although there were very creditable entries from five under 3-acre gardens, and not just in the classes reserved specially for them.

Classes 1 and 2, for the large flowered group of species and hybrids, provided the best spectacle, with first and second prizes in Class 1 going to Borde Hill for a beautiful flower of *M. campbellii alba* and a good pink *M. sprengeri* seedling, respectively. Another *M. campbellii alba*, from Maurice Foster, was a close third.

Class 2, for sprays, was the most visually electrifying, with first prize – and best in show – going to a superb spray of 'Caerhays Surprise' by Maurice Foster (see below). A

MICHAEL SHUTTLEWORTH

Maurice Foster's *Magnolia* 'Caerhays Surprise', winner of Class 2

Borde Hill spray of a *sprengeri* seedling was a close second, with Exbury showing 'Athene' for third place.

Only one spray of 'Butterflies' made it into the Acuminata Class 3, and even that was not fully out. However, it gave Maurice Foster another first! Maurice dominated Class 4 as well, with first for a *M. denudata* seedling and second for his own hybrid, 'Theodora'. Exbury took third with 'Sundew'.

Class 5 gave Maurice Foster more points, with one of the small garden entries of a 'Leonard Messel', by Barry Haseltine, creeping into third place.

Classes 9 and 10 saw the most competition from the small gardens, although the Bristow family dominated in Class 9 with Anthony winning first with a very good flower of a seedling of, probably, *M. sargentiana* var. *robusta*, named for the show as 'Bill Saucell' – a huge pure white, and second with another of his seedlings, again specially named, 'Chantal'. His son, Nick gained third prize with 'Jane Platt'. Brian Wright took long enough away from his rhododendrons and camellias to win first in Class 10 with a spray of 'Leonard Messel', and Tim Graham cleaned up the other two prizes with 'Galaxy' and *M. stellata* var. *rosea*. Tim also pipped Anthony Bristow for the prize for the best small garden effort.

It was no surprise to find that Maurice Foster had retained the trophy for the best overall performance in the Magnolia Competition, a fitting result, as his entries had contributed so much to its success, in spite of the lateness of the spring.

Barry Haseltine

AWARDS

Two camellias both sent by Trehane Camellia Nursery and assessed on Battleston Hill were granted the Award of Garden Merit – AGM (H4).

***Camellia* 'Clarrie Fawcett'**
'Virtually no petal blight or frost damage. Good shape, colour and habit, compact, pure pale warm pink. Very free flowering, showing up well against the leaves.' Available from Loder Plants and the Duchy of Cornwall Nursery.

***Camellia* 'Elizabeth Anderson'**
'Nice form. Shatters well. Soft rose double. Very special. An excellent plant'. Available from Loder Plants.

Camellia 'Clarrie Fawcett' (above)
Camellia 'Elizabeth Anderson' (below)

RHS Rhododendron and Camellia Committee

Chairman
Dr M L A Robinson, Hindhead Lodge, Priory Road, Forest Row, E Sussex RH18 5JF
Email: mlarob@hotmail.com

Vice-Chairman vacancy

Secretary
Dr D Edwards, RHS Garden Wisley, Woking, Surrey GU23 6QB
Email: dawnedwards@rhs.org.uk

Members
C Fairweather, Beacon Gate, Beaulieu, Hampshire SO42 7YR
Email: christopher@fairweather.co.uk

M Flanagan, Verderers, Wick Road, Englefield Green, Egham, Surrey TW20 3AE
Email: mark.flanagan@theroyallandscape.co.uk

M C Foster, White House Farm, Ivy Hatch, Sevenoaks, Kent TN15 0NN
Email: RosiFoster@aol.com

J T Gallagher, Oldfield, 29 Moorlands Road, Verwood, Dorset BH31 6PD
Email: magnolianut@hotmail.com

A F George, Hydon Nurseries, Hydon Heath, Godalming, Surrey GU8 4AZ

J G Hillier, c/o Hillier Nurseries, Ampfield House, Ampfield, Romsey, Hants SO51 9PA
Email: john_hillier@hillier.co.uk

Dr R H L Jack, Edgemoor, Loch Road, Lanark ML11 9BG

T Methuen-Campbell, Penrice Castle, Reynoldston, Swansea, West Glamorgan SA3 1LN

D G Millais, Crosswater Farm, Churt, Farnham, Surrey GU10 2JN
Email: sales@rhododendrons.co.uk

M Pharoah, Lower Tithe Barn, Marwood, Barnstaple, Devon EX31 4EB
Email: malcolmpharoah@supanet.com

A W SIMONS, Wingfield House, 11 Brinsmade Road, Ampthill, Bedfordshire
Email: a.simons@ntlworld.com

A V SKINNER, MBE, 2 Frog Firle Cottage, Alfriston, nr Polegate, E Sussex BN26 5TT

M O SLOCOCK, VMH, Hillside Cottage, Brentmoor Road, West End, Woking, Surrey GU24 9ND

C B TOMLIN, Starborough Nursery, Starborough Road, Marsh Green, Edenbridge, Kent TN8 5RB

Miss J TREHANE, 353 Church Cottages, Hampreston, Wimborne, Dorset BH21 7LX
Email: jennifer@trehane.co.uk

C H WILLIAMS, Burncoose Nurseries, Gwennap, Redruth, Cornwall TR16 6BJ
Email: diana@burncoose.co.uk

RHS Rhododendron, Camellia and Magnolia Group

Officers

Chairman Dr M L A Robinson, Hindleap Lodge, Priory Road, Forest Row, E Sussex RH18 5JF (Tel: 01342 822745, Email: mlarob@hotmail.com)

Vice Chairman Mr Philip D Evans, West Netherton, Drewsteignton, Devon EX6 6RB (Tel/fax: 01647 281285, Email: philip.d.evans@talk21.com)

Hon. Treasurer Mr Martin D C Gates, 12 Marlborough Road, Chandlers Ford, Eastleigh, Hants SO53 5DH (Tel: 023 8025 2843)

Hon. Secretary Mrs Pat Bucknell, Botallick, Lanreath, Looe, Cornwall PL13 2PF (Tel: 01503 220215, Email: PatBucknell@tiscali.co.uk)

Hon. Membership Secretary Mr Rupert L C Eley, East Bergholt Place, East Bergholt, Suffolk CO7 6UP (Tel/fax: 01206 299224, Email: sales@placeforplants.co.uk)

Hon. Yearbook Editor Mr Philip D Evans, West Netherton, Drewsteignton, Devon EX6 6RB (Tel/fax: 01647 281285, Email: philip.d.evans@talk21.com)

Hon. Bulletin Editor Mr John A Rawling, The Spinney, Station Road, Woldingham, Surrey CR3 7DD (Tel: 01883 653341, Email: jr.eye@virgin.net)

Yearbook Archivist Pam Hayward, Woodtown, Sampford Spiney, Yelverton, Devon PL20 6LJ (Tel/fax: 01822 852122, Email: pam@woodtown.net)

Hon. Tours Organiser Mrs Judy Hallett, Bryher, The Common, Potten End, Berkhamsted, Hertfordshire HP4 2QF (Tel: 01442 865914, Email: judy.hallett@googlemail.com)

Webmaster Mr Graham Mills, Tregoning Mill, St Keverne, Helston, Cornwall TR12 6QE (Tel: 01326 280382, Fax: 0871 4337066, Email: graham@tregoningmill.co.uk)

Committee Members

Mr Eric Annal, 36 Hillview Crescent, Edinburgh EH12 8QG (Tel: 0131 334 2574, Fax: 0131 334 6191, Email: eric.annal@btinternet.com)

Mr Maurice C Foster, White House Farm, Ivy Hatch, Sevenoaks, Kent TN15 0NN (Tel: 01732 810634, Fax: 01732 810553, Email: RosiFoster@aol.com)

Mr John D Harsant, Newton House, Well Lane, Heswall, Wirral, Merseyside CH60 8NF (Tel: 0151 342 3664, Fax: 0151 348 4015, Email: john@harsant.uk.com (Publicity Officer)

Mr Andy Simons, Wingfield House, 11 Brimsmade Road, Ampthill, Bedfordshire MK45 2PP (Tel: 01525 753398, Email: a.simons@ntlworld.com)

Mr Alastair T STEVENSON, Appledore, Upton Bishop, Ross-on-Wye, Herefordshire HR9 7UL
(Tel: 01989 780285, Fax: 01989 780591, Email: alastairstevenson@tiscali.co.uk
(Co-ordinator of Events and Publicity Officer)
Mr Ivor T STOKES, Llyshendy, Llandeilo, Carmarthenshire SA19 6YA
(Tel/fax: 01558 823233, Email: ivor.stokes@btopenworld.com)
Mr Brian E WRIGHT, Kilsaran, Fielden Lane, Crowborough, Sussex TN6 1TL
(Tel: 01892 653207, Fax: 01892 669550, Email: iriswright@msn.com)

Branch Chairmen
International Mrs Miranda GUNN, Ramster, Petworth Road, Chiddingfold, Surrey GU8 4SN
(Tel: 01428 644422, Fax: 01428 658345, Email: Ramsterweddings@tiscali.co.uk)
New Forest Mr Christopher FAIRWEATHER, The Garden Centre, High Street, Beaulieu, Hants
SO42 7YR (Tel: 01590 612307, Fax: 01590 612519, Email: chrisfairweather@waitrose.com)
Norfolk Vacancy
North Wales and Northwest Mr C E J BRABIN, Rosewood, Puddington Village, Neston
CH64 5SS (Tel: 0151 353 1193, Email: angela.brabin@tesco.net)
Peak District Dr David R IVES, 18 Park Road, Birstall, Leicestershire LE4 3AU
(Tel: 0116 2675118, Email: rosidavid.ives@btopenworld.com)
Southeast Mr Barry HASELTINE, Goodwins, Snow Hill, Crawley Down, Sussex
RH10 3EF (Tel: 01342 713132, Email: barry.haseltine@which.net)
Southwest Mr Colin H T BROWN, West Winds, Lustleigh, Newton Abbot, Devon
TQ13 9TR (Tel: 01647 277268, Email: marylou@lustleigh.plus.com)
Ulster Mr Patrick FORDE, Seaforde, Downpatrick, Co Down BT30 8PG
(Tel: 01396 811225, Fax: 01396 811370, Email: Plants@SeafordeGardens.com)
Wessex Mrs Miranda GUNN, Ramster, Petworth Road, Chiddingfold, Surrey GU8 4SN
(Tel: 01428 644422, Fax: 01428 658345, email: Ramsterweddings@tiscali.co.uk)

Convenor of Group Seed Bank Mr Gerald J DIXON, Brooklands, Shute, Axminster, Devon
EX13 7QF (Tel: 01404 831689, Fax: 01404 831552,
Email: brooklandrhododendrons@btinternet.com)

Membership: for details of Membership please contact the Hon. Membership Secretary

Website addresses: rhodogroup-rhs.org magnoliasociety.org vireya.net

Index